ILLUSTRATING Children's BOOKS

ILLUSTRATING Children's BOOKS

Martin Ursell

THE CROWOOD PRESS

First published in 2013 by
The Crowood Press Ltd
Ramsbury, Marlborough
Wiltshire SN8 2HR

www.crowood.com

British Library Cataloguing-in-Publication Data
A catalogue record for this book is available from the British Library.

ISBN 978 1 84797 433 4

Frontispiece: *The Last Stronghold*, Martin Ursell

Dedication

Dedicated to John Dowling, keep that lamp shining!

Typeset by Sharon Dainton, Isis Design.
Printed and bound in India by Replika Press Pvt Ltd.

CONTENTS

FOREWORD

I first met Martin Ursell when I was teaching on the BA Illustration course at Chelsea School of Art and he was a new student. The Head of Department came into the staff-room and announced, 'At last! We have a real illustrator on our course.'

'Who is it?' I asked, eager to make contact.

'I'm not going to tell you that,' she replied. 'You will have to discover him for yourself.'

And I did. As soon as he walked into the studio, with his sketchbooks under his arm, and sat down to draw, there was never any doubt.

Since those student days Martin Ursell has gone on to become a well-loved illustrator and author in every area of children's books and picture books. He is also an inspiring teacher with an exceptional ability to discover the potential in every student. He started his teaching career at Chelsea and now is head of Second Year Illustration at Middlesex University and a lecturer at Kingston University.

This book is the product of Martin's experience over the years both in publishing and as a teacher. Aspiring illustrators will find everything they need to know about how to put together a portfolio of work to show a publisher. There is excellent advice on keeping sketchbooks, on drawing from memory and on location, and on using reference. In addition there is practical advice on every aspect of illustration, from what materials to use to the technical requirements of the 32-page picture book and to the different needs of the longer illustrated book and the graphic novel.

The exercises and projects in this book are carefully constructed to take the reader through a complete course in book illustration. They will stimulate your imagination, help you to generate ideas, and develop your understanding of the vital link between text and image that is central to illustrating books.

Carolyn Dinan

Carolyn Dinan, RCA

LEFT: Drawing ink.

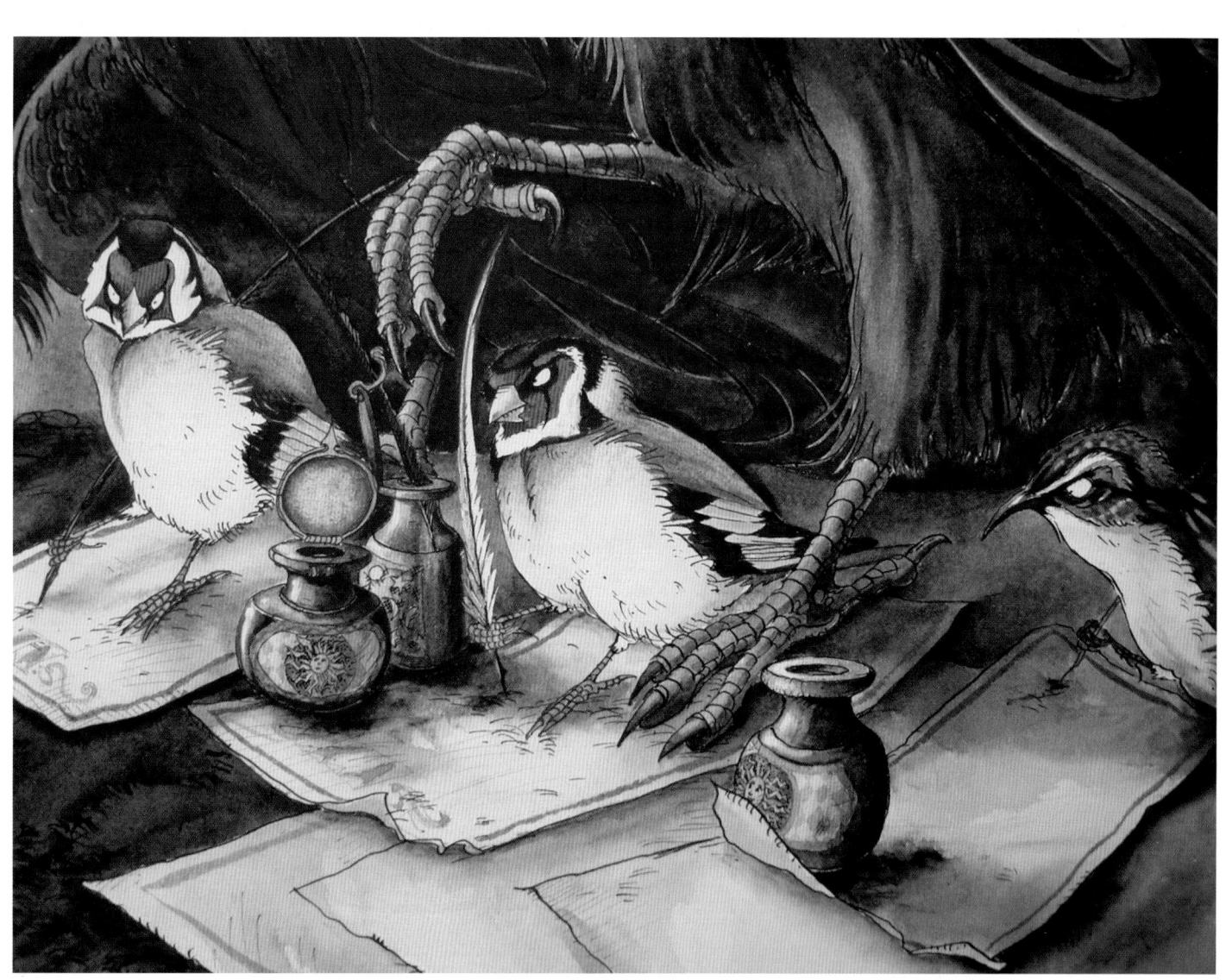

INTRODUCTION

There have been stories and pictures describing important, marvellous or traumatic events in the lives of civilizations going back as far as we are able to see. However, it was not really until the nineteenth century that books with pictures, specifically for children, were created in any quantity and even then it was not until the end of that century that this medium really began to take off. This was in part due to developments in printing processes and techniques but it was also due to a change in attitudes to children and their place in society. The great advances made in the nineteenth and early twentieth centuries in literacy among children and a gradual breaking down of class barriers offering education to most of the population also helped create a ready market for books for children.

Today one can visit any bookstore and choose a children's book from shelf upon shelf of picture books; there are even entire shops specializing just in the stocking and selling of books for children. The children's publishing world meets in Bologna, Italy, each spring where thousands of children's books jostle and compete for attention and recognition. Now with advances in printing and the availability through the Internet of extremely competitive deals for self publishing it is probably easier than at any other time in history to produce and publish your own children's book. So how does one go about this?

Well, of course, one needs to have an idea. This idea will need to be explored and developed through sketchbook work and the feeding in of knowledge garnered from reference material. Characters need to be created and developed so that they communicate exactly what it is that you intend. Next, these rough ideas and drawings will need to be processed into a 'dummy' book so that one can see exactly, in rough, what this book could be like before investing hours and money in producing the illustrations for real.

Then one needs to think how to make the illustrations: what materials will be best to use, what paper, how big should the illustrations be, how many should one have and how should they be created? How will printing affect the way one produces these illustrations and how should the pictures and story be combined?

Once the book is going well, how does one go about finding a publisher to publish this book and at what moment does one approach a publisher?

Exactly how one can successfully accomplish all of these tasks is the substance of the following pages. In writing about how to illustrate books for children I have tried to give this task a natural continuity but this does not mean it is the only way to do it. Different illustrators work in various ways and there is not one single correct way of achieving this goal. However, what follows is a logical way of making a children's book and a way that works.

Throughout the book a variety of successful children's illustrators are profiled; they talk about how they go about writing and illustrating their own books, each discussing their specific influences and how they manage to find inspiration and sustain their motivation through to the end of a project. Looking at how other illustrators go about the task of making an image or working on a piece of artwork can be inspiring and encouraging; looking at the variety of media and methods they employ reinforces the myriad ways of going about illustrating a book.

At the end of each chapter there are projects and exercises designed to help the illustrator work in a creative and productive way. Each project relates specifically to the subject matter of the chapter, and as a whole the projects can be viewed as a mini-course in illustrating a children's book.

There is no mystery to illustrating a children's book. It is not something only someone who has been good at art from the age of one month can do but it is something that calls for a great deal of commitment. Wanting, really wanting, to illustrate a picture book is half the battle. Having a good idea but more importantly recognizing a good idea from a cliché is another must. Some confidence in yourself and your ability is useful and being disciplined and motivated is essential: one does not usually undertake and complete a project of this nature without the odd hurdle or three. Try not to give up too easily and try to be receptive to suggestions and advice. It is difficult to look again at work when one has spent ages, maybe days, on it but the amount of time spent on something is no guarantee of quality – one can just as easily achieve this in a five-second drawing which for no discernible reason somehow just works!

I enjoy the entire process of illustrating a picture book and could not choose between drawing the roughs, going out with a sketchbook, working on the dummy or making the artwork as my favourite activity; I love doing it all. I hope you find this book useful and that it helps you on the way to illustrating your own picture book.

Martin Ursell.

These initial sketches by Wesley Robins are full of interest, excitement and enthusiasm. The details of the bags and clothing make one immediately eager to see the book that they inspired. A bizarre small drawing of a Zulu shield and spear add to the atmosphere of Victoriana, as does the mounted and stuffed deer head. Even on this page of the earliest ideas for his book Wesley has already convinced us that this book will be a winner.

Chapter One
HAVING AN
IDEA

There is no way of starting a picture book without having an idea. Try not to be daunted by this. An idea can come from anywhere: a phrase, a character, an incident, an image, even a joke. The story can be developed from this starting point – in fact that is exactly what making a picture book is – and one does not expect to begin the project with everything already sorted out.

Of course, you might want to use a story that already exists. Fairy tales, nursery rhymes, and fables all make for good starting points. You do not need to keep exactly to the original telling, and there is no knowing how they might evolve. Therefore, the Aesop's fable of *The Boy Who Cried Wolf* might become the story of a naughty Edwardian girl named Matilda who repeatedly shouts 'Fire!' though there is no fire, until when there is a fire and she shouts, nobody comes and she is burnt to death, as in Hilaire Belloc's famous poem.

Your idea might be to have a counting book, or an alphabet book or a book about colours or shapes. The book may not have a story at all but be told by pictures alone. It may be telling us how to look after a pet or how to tell the difference between good and bad. These are all starting points.

If you are planning to have a go at writing your own story the first thing to remember is that it is a picture book; you do not really want there to be too much text or there will not be enough room for the pictures. Most picture books are 32 pages long (we will discuss this in more detail in Chapter 5), so a maximum of one thousand words – far fewer than it sounds – is a reasonable aim to start with.

In children's picture books, many of the same basic plots are used again and again. The brilliance of the book is in the creativity of the author and the illustrator breathing new life into these themes. You may find the following list of the most commonly used themes useful as a trigger for your imagination.

- A story based on a window, door or portal into another world. For example, *Alice in Wonderland*, *The Narnia Chronicles*, *The Subtle Knife*.
- An untrustworthy character who tricks or gets the better of the other characters. For example Brer Rabbit, *Mr and Mrs Pig's Evening Out*.

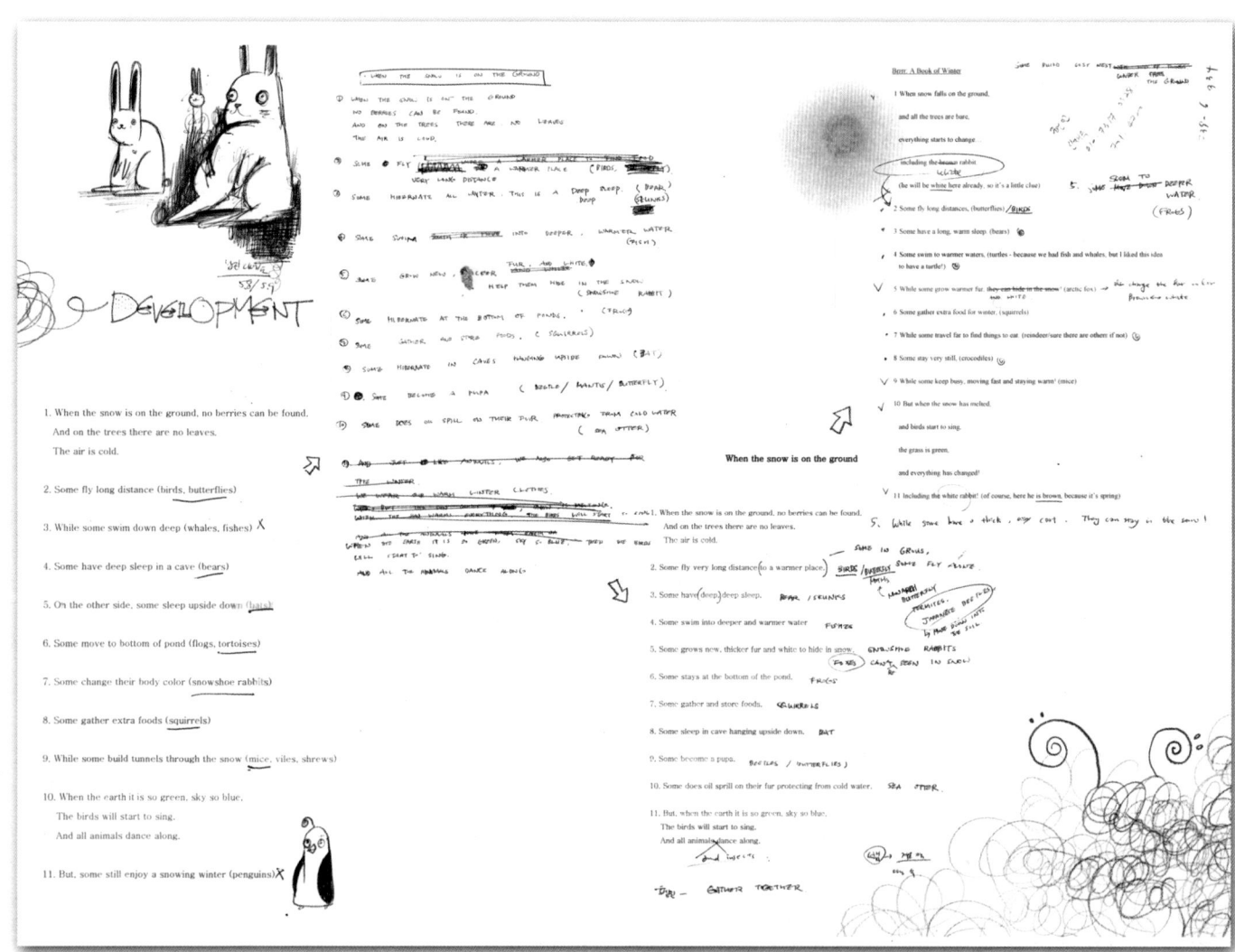

- A child who is mistaken for someone else.
- A character who is lost, either literally or metaphorically.
- A dream world where on falling asleep the character is somewhere else.
- The character having a fear of something that is resolved by the end of the book. They are shy, small or different.
- A riddle or a puzzle that needs solving. For example, *Where's Wally?*, *The Ultimate Zoo*.
- Dealing with a catastrophe or disaster.
- An inanimate object that becomes real. For example, *The Velveteen Rabbit*, *Pinocchio*.
- A powerful being or monster that the child helps, with the result that they become friends.
- Curiosity, good or bad. For example, *Pandora's Box*, *Curious George*.
- Dealing with a strange or eccentric family member.
- A magic implement or a spell that seems marvellous, only to end in tears. For example, *Sparky's Magic Piano*, *King Midas*.
- A story about sharing, either with a positive outcome or a negative one. For example, *The Fiends*, *The Dog in the Manger*.
- A character taken out of their element to experience the consequences. For example, *The Town Mouse and the Country Mouse*, *The Fox and the Stork*.
- A vice or bad habit that leads to problems. For example, *The Tale of Timmy Tiptoes*.
- A chain of events where one thing leads to the next like a series of consequences.
- A chosen one or special child. For example *The Sword in the Stone*, *Harry Potter*.

These ideas sheets for Il Sung Na's *Brrr: A Book of Winter* begin as no more than thoughts and words. The doodles and scribbles gradually evolve into more definite ideas for an illustrated picture book but one is left with a clear idea, looking at these sheets, that the book might go down any number of different routes. Keeping your options open in these early stages is very important.

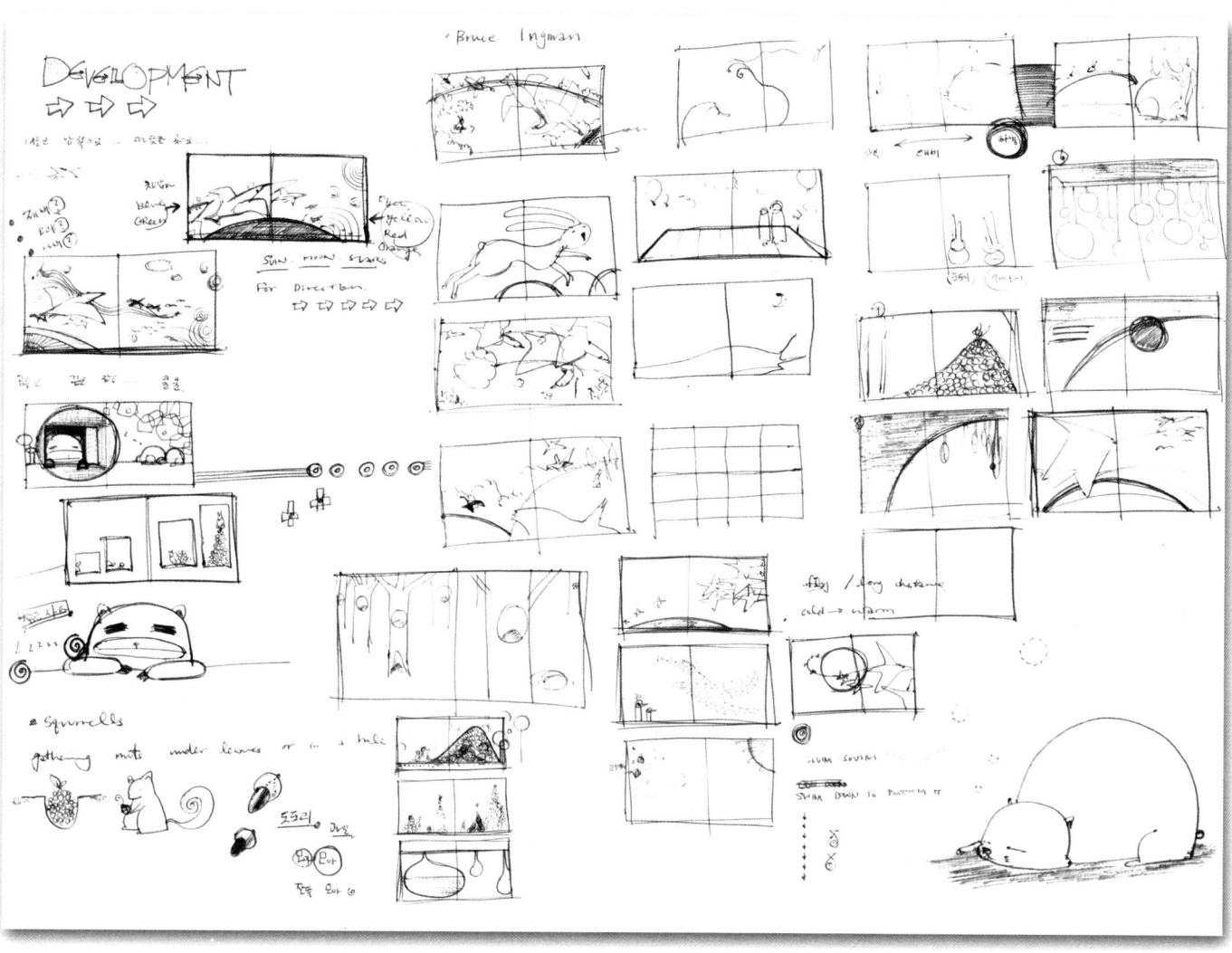

Emma Block is looking at the Grimm brothers' tale of *Hansel and Gretel* with these sketchbook studies. She is imagining what the characters might wear, what kind of world they might live in and who might share that world with them – forest animals, for example. In these very early stages of a picture book it is vital to cover this kind of ground. Inevitably, many of these ideas will never metamorphose into full-blown picture books but it is at this stage that one explores the possibilities.

It is no good waiting for inspiration to strike. One must set out to have an idea. Keeping a sketchbook or notebook of things that interest you or just things that happen is a great way of creating a source that you can refer to in order to get the imagination going. Often the best ideas occur whilst one is too busy to do anything with them so write them down where you will be able to find them. Like all these things this is something that happens over time, not something that one can do in an afternoon.

There are many ways of starting with an idea and developing this into a picture book and, as is the case with much of illustration, different ways work for different illustrators. Here are a few suggestions as to how to develop an idea.

- Beginning with an idea based on personal experience is a good start, maybe an episode or interesting adventure; write it out or draw it out as a storyboard, exactly as it happened. Now look at what you have and re-imagine those parts of the story that are dull or unnecessary – remember you do not have to keep to the facts. Think of it like retelling an anecdote: in order to make the story more interesting one often exaggerates a little or embellishes a few details. Try doing this with your visuals. In the same way, when one is recounting a story verbally one might want to give the characters different voices, or talk faster or louder at particular points of your tale. One can do the same thing with visuals by drawing lots of small drawings instead of one large image, or by choosing a bold dramatic angle to illustrate and emphasize a particular character's action. When starting an idea the thing is to try everything. Explore and experiment all

CAN YOU SPOT THE DIFFERENCE? FIND 14 CHANGES!

Spot the difference by Rina Donnersmarck.

the time and try not to settle for the first image that comes into your head. It often seems like this is the best image one can come up with but there is almost always a much better idea just around the corner. This last point is extremely important and worth noting down.

- A joke makes another good starting point. It might need some work to turn this into a full picture book but on the other hand one already has the punch line to the story and this is often one of the most difficult things to resolve. As before, draw out your story in quick, simple visuals or roughs. At this stage try not to worry too much about using reference – this comes later; more important now is getting a feel for how one tells a story. Is it interesting and are you keeping the reader's attention? Usually in a picture book one does not have many pages to tell the story so every word and image has to count. When beginning and developing an idea into a series of pictures try to make the reader really want to turn the page each time.

- Starting an idea with a character is perhaps a more unusual beginning but it is a method used by many illustrators. It works like this. Start with a drawing of a character, based on someone drawn directly from observation, or from reference or from your imagination. Where might this character live? Visualize this. What kind of place would this be? What kind of things would they have? What kind of work might they do? What might happen to your character? Many illustrators produce sketchbooks full of drawings that explore these questions. Gradually a visual dossier will emerge from which one should be able to piece together a story. It is just the same as noticing someone in the street and imagining what kind of life they might have working from the clues available – what they wear, what shopping they buy, whether they have a pet, how they walk, and so on.

- Beginning with an existing story has the advantage that the storyline and ending are already sorted out so you will not have to spend ages trying to think of a surprise ending. If you are using an old fairy tale or fable you can update this by setting it in the present day or just somewhere else, changing the characters' names and where the action takes place to give the story a new flavour. You are free also to alter the direction that the original story takes. Therefore you might heighten the excitement in a well known story by going against the normal course of events; for example, what would happen if in the famous Brothers Grimm story of Snow White she never ate the apple, or if the dwarves were not kind, charming eccentrics but malevolent, threatening characters. Remember using an existing story is yet another starting point and it may develop in any direction, so much so that the original story or starting point is lost and forgotten. If you are planning to use a more recent story then it is important to be aware of potential copyright issues.

Many picture books are created around issues that children may experience, for example, bullying, shyness, being small, not wanting to eat healthy food, even the death of a pet or someone close. These subjects make challenging but pertinent starting points and give the picture book a point in enabling a child, through the book, to learn how to deal with these issues and problems.

In recent years there has been much emphasis on this aspect of a picture book and in some cases it can make for a 'preachy' or 'worthy' book. Try not to get bogged down with issues like this. Writing and illustrating a children's picture book is a long project that demands a great deal of time, work and effort. It is best to start with an idea that you are interested in and produce a book that you would want to read.

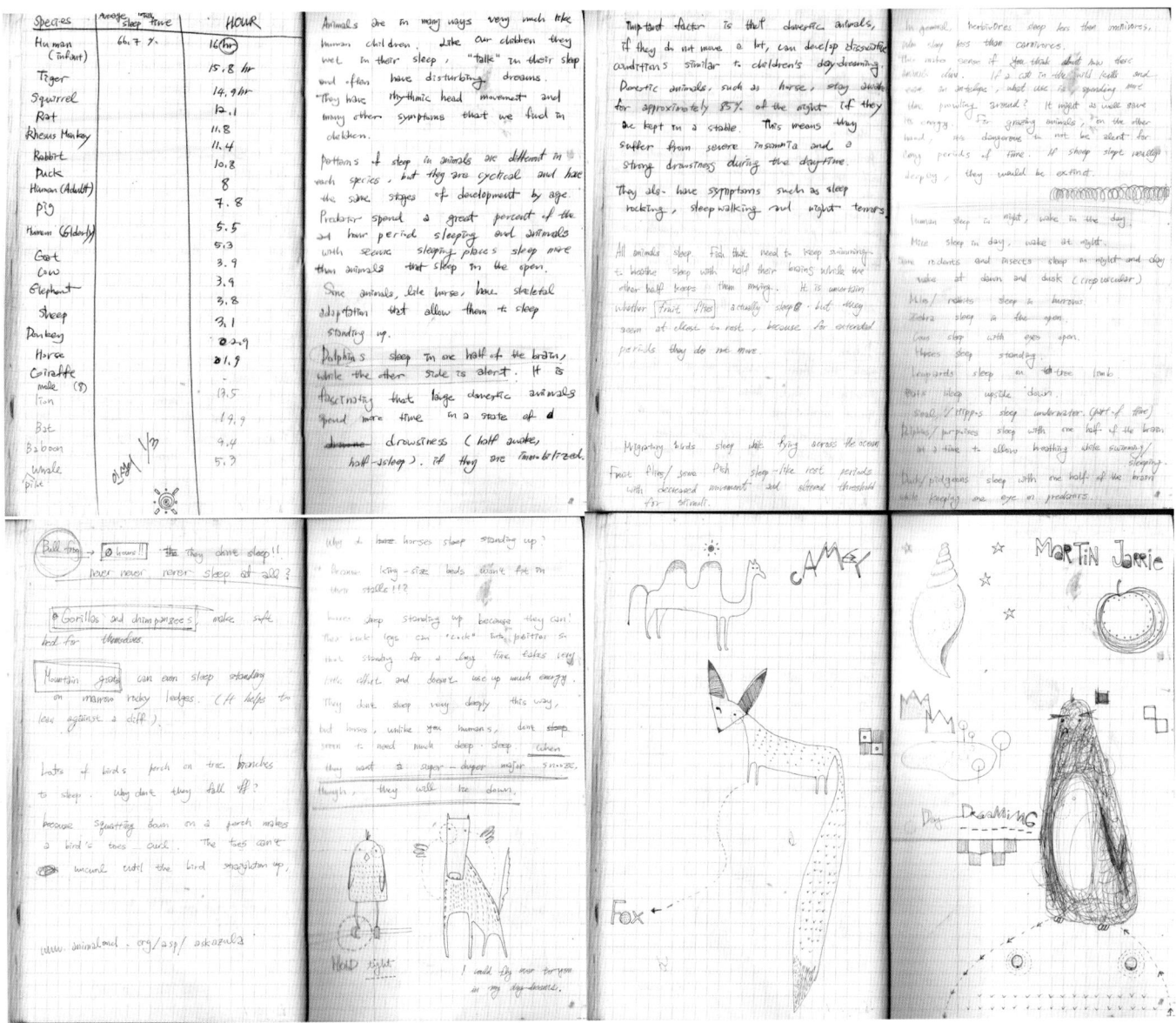

These ideas sheets by Il Sung Na for his picture book *ZZzzz: A Book of Sleep* show how, from his initial ideas that are mainly written, he is gradually developing the book through doodles, character sketches and small visuals. Notice how Il Sung's first ideas are notes and words. The foundation of the book is about the variety of ways in which animals sleep and you can see clearly how, as he researches his ideas and finds out exactly how different animals go about this, his imagination is triggered to produce illustration.

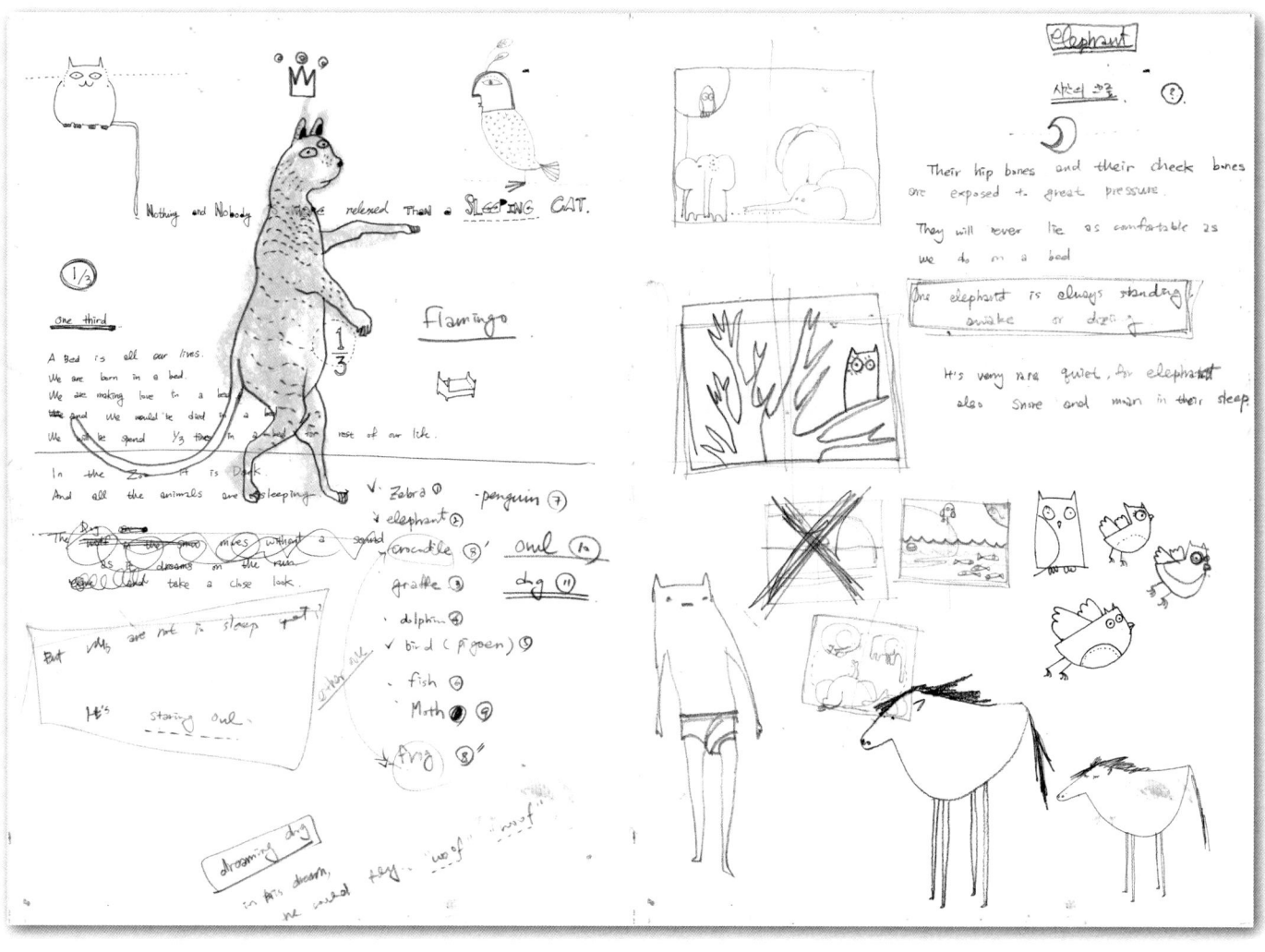

The record of how long different animals sleep for helps him decide which animals to include in the book. Drawing them and giving them character also helps in this task. Il Sung is thinking not only of which animals will be the most interesting to include because of how they sleep but also of which will make for a varied and colourful group.
Deciding which animals to include will, to some extent, dictate how the illustrations are made.

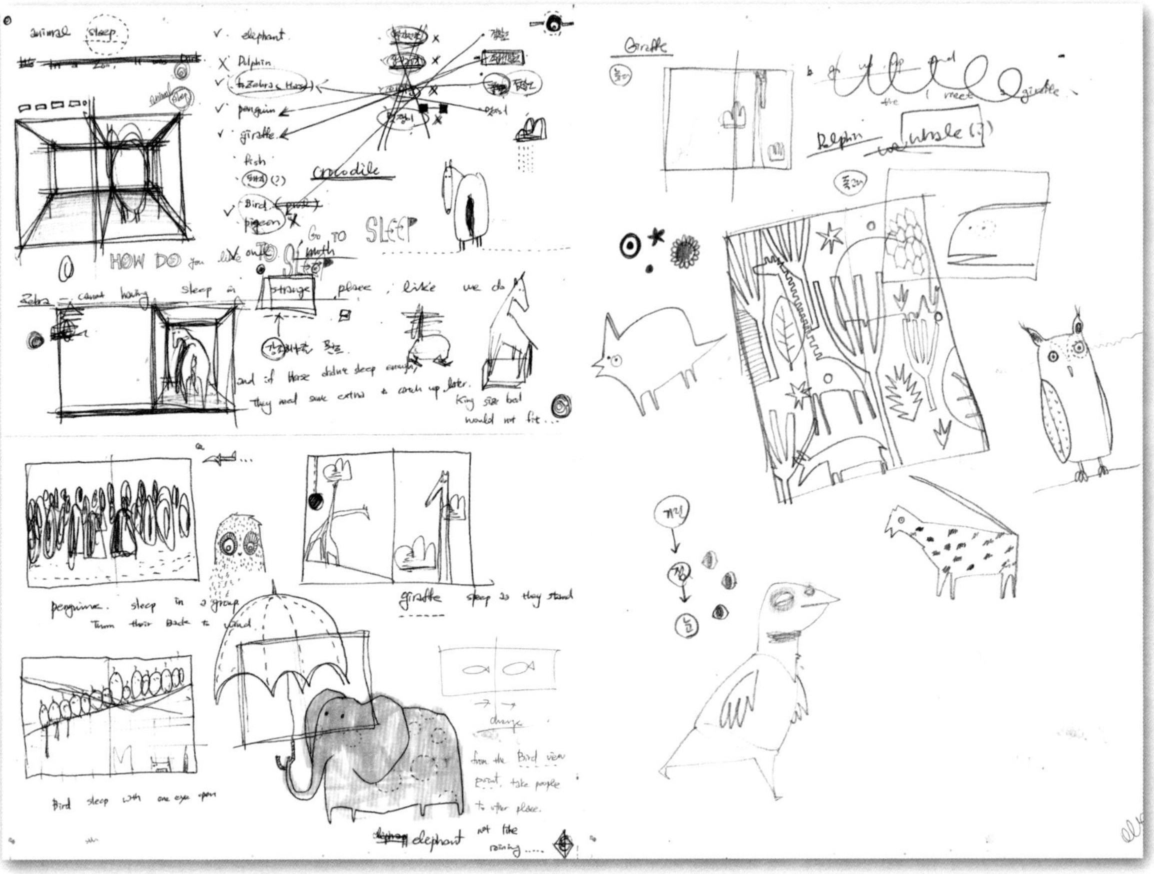

Do all of the animals come from the same country? Is this of any relevance to the story? Are they to wear clothes? How like real animals should they be and is this of any importance to the story? These are all questions that lead on from an initial idea. Notice how even at this early stage of his book Il Sung is already thinking in terms of these drawings being enclosed by the page. The design and composition in all of Il Sung's books is always a very strong element and it is no wonder when this is given consideration almost from the very beginning.

The House of Fairy Tales by Rina Donnersmarck.

WORKING WITH A PARTNER

You may feel that making the pictures is the thing that you do best and that creating a story is not your forte. Most illustrators would see themselves in this category and it is a rare illustrator who can write and illustrate equally well. There is no denying that the story is very important, probably more important than the pictures as, usually, picture books are read to a child then turned so that the child can see the pictures. However, the pictures are what we remember, and it is through the pictures that we enter into a different world, a world created by the illustrator.

Collaborating with a writer can be a great way to produce a book if you do not feel confident enough with your writing ability. There is also the consideration that you may well be able to write a good story but one that would be better suited to an illustrator other than yourself. Most illustrators have specific subject matter and scenarios that they are comfortable illustrating. For example, Beatrix Potter is unsurpassed in her portrayal of animals and their worlds but readily admitted struggling greatly when introducing people into her stories. For this reason she avoided introducing people into her stories but may well have had a whole collection of great stories all to do with people. This would have been a great opportunity for collaboration with a partner.

Which comes first: the story or the pictures? Usually the story would come first and the illustrator would respond with pictures only when the story was complete. This does not mean the story cannot change and it may still evolve while the illustrator is working on the roughs. However, it can also work the other way around: a writer taking a completed set of illustrations and writing a story to go with them.

These little line drawings by Rina Donnersmarck might get up to any number of adventures. Many illustrators begin stories by creating simple characters like this.

PROFILE: IL SUNG NA

The Korean illustrator Il Sung Na writes and illustrates his own picture books and talks here about how he generates ideas for books like *ZZzzz: A Book of Sleep, Brrr: A Book of Winter* and *Hide and Seek*.

I always keep a notebook with me. I think this is extremely important as I can have an idea anywhere – on the bus, eating a meal or just before going to sleep – and if I don't write it down I will forget it. I need to record this idea so that I can consider it when there is time. Sitting and staring at a blank sheet of paper does not work for me at all. I would rather go outside and search for ideas. When I have an idea I think and think around it, trying to determine whether it is a good idea worth working on or whether it is a cliché. I write first, making notes and sentences in my sketchbook, maybe I am writing the end or the middle or a rough storyline. I will come back to all of this later to see if I am still interested. I may sometimes doodle around these words and sentences but usually only if I have a rough idea for an image. I might begin character studies at this stage.

I get most of my ideas from real life experiences. For instance the idea for *Brrr: A Book of Winter* came to me on a freezing cold day when I had just moved back from London to Seoul. It was so cold I ended up putting on several layers of warm sweaters and jumpers and the thought popped into my head, how did animals manage to keep warm in winter? I knew that some animals migrated and that some hibernated but I also knew that a lot did neither of these things and I thought there might be a book here.

ZZzzz: A Book of Sleep was similar. I was just going off to sleep when I suddenly thought how different animals sleep. I got up and wrote on a piece of paper, 'sleep and animals'. The next day I researched how different animals sleep in so many different ways and I knew I could make a story from this.

Keeping your eyes and ears wide open you can observe so many things. Always asking how something happens or why, these are good starting points. It is difficult to know if you have a good idea

Il Sung Na.

or maybe a non-starter and perhaps this is a decision for someone else. I think if an idea makes me curious then it might interest someone else but I also think an idea shouldn't be too personal. It has to be an idea that people can share in and relate to.

The roughs are the most important part of working on a book; for me this is also the most difficult part. Working out the flow of a book, knowing when to make a calmer simpler page, working on the compositions, there'll be a lot of re-working and re-doing here but if I don't get the roughs right then it doesn't matter how good my artwork is, it will never shine.

I like colouring the artwork best and use anything and everything. I have no preference for certain media and use pens, pencils, acrylic, pastels, the computer – I don't care if it is expensive or cheap paint: what matters is how I use it. I'm not saying this part is easy, I don't think any part of working on a book is easy, but I do find this stage a little more enjoyable than other parts.

I can spend a year on a book and may be

working on several different projects at the same time. I make a time schedule for myself and I stick to it. If you are a full-time author and illustrator then you need to keep your life going as well.

It is very difficult to publish your book. Finding the right publisher involves a lot of effort and a tough skin. Some publishers don't reply, some reply that they don't like your book but hopefully some do like your work. As an illustrator you need to have a good business mind too. If you sit and do nothing then you will never get commissioned to do work; you need to regularly promote yourself.

Although I enjoyed drawing when I was young I never thought of being an illustrator but instead wanted to be an architect and build my own house. When I came to London and went to art school I gradually became more and more interested in illustration. I spent most of my free time in bookshops looking at all the children's books and gradually although I did not know if I could manage to become a children's book illustrator and author I knew I wanted to try.

My favourite illustrators are Shaun Tan and Alexis Deacon because I think their story telling is as good as their illustrations. I like Sara Fanelli, Henrik Drescher and lately Oliver Jeffers. There are many more and if you want I can name a dozen more!

PROJECT ONE:
IMAGINING A STORY FROM A PHOTOGRAPH

Start with an old family photograph or a photograph from a magazine. Reproduce this image, through drawing, in your sketchbook. Now imagine what might have happened when the photographer had finished. Where did the subjects go? What happened to them next? Feel free to use your imagination. It may be they just walked into a different room or went for a meal, or changed into more ordinary clothes from the special clothes they had put on for the photograph. It maybe that an escaped leopard suddenly leapt through the window or that the characters were suddenly shrunken down, or grew moustaches, or sprouted wings. Whatever you imagine happens, draw it. Fill your sketchbook with this evolving scenario. There is no need to worry about how it might end. Maybe you introduce new characters who take the story in a different direction. Try to complete the sketchbook this way.

When your sketchbook is complete, look at what you have. In another book or by photocopying your drawings, edit and reassemble the best bits of your story, adding new drawings where you feel it does not quite work. At this stage you are looking to tighten and heighten the drama and narrative of your story. Add speech bubbles and words if you feel it will help the story.

PROJECT TWO:
A CHILDHOOD MEMORY

Think back to your childhood; maybe you had an annoying sibling or felt strongly over a particular issue, for example, a food you would not eat or was a favourite, a particularly odd relative, lucky socks or a phobia. Make lists of these memories. Do not be tempted to leave off those that you think are not good enough; put them all down. By writing them down you have got rid of them and can think of something else.

Now look at your list and choose the five anecdotes that seem to you the most interesting. Draw out the story very simply, again using speech bubbles but trying to make the drawings tell the story. Feel free to add and embellish the story to make it more interesting. If in real life it did not end in the way you would wish, now is your chance to give this memory the ending you would have liked.

PROJECT THREE:
VARIATIONS ON A THEME

Create an image. As an example to illustrate this project we will use a bird on a nest. Draw the bird sitting on its nest. In a second drawing draw the same image from a different point of view, maybe from the point of view of the egg. Now again but perhaps from the point of view of a cat watching the bird on its nest. Continue with this exercise until you feel you have exhausted its possibilities. You are not developing this story as we did in the first project, but imagining different ways of showing the initial image that might indicate where the story could go. You should have at least forty different images of your starting point. Again, keep your drawings quick and very simple: we are concerned with getting ideas down, not with making beautiful pictures. This comes later.

Chapter Two
SKETCHBOOKS

Keeping a sketchbook, drawing in it every day, recording what you see around you and noting down, either visually or with words, ideas and thoughts that may occur to you, is probably the single most useful and productive thing to do when thinking of starting a children's book. Keeping a sketchbook is and should be a habit; the more you do it the more you will be able to do it and you will find that a library of ideas, reference and observations will accrue without you really noticing. It is very difficult to come up with a good idea on demand and sketchbooks can be invaluable in prompting the memory to be imaginative.

By recording everyday life and thoughts in a sketchbook one is continually creating and adding to a store, a collection of starting points that may be developed and explored later. Many of the best picture books start like this. The sketchbook is

also a great place to gather reference, drawing from life the things that appear in your story for later use.

There is no single 'right' way of keeping a sketchbook. Different illustrators and artists will keep their sketchbooks in different ways. It may be that a small bound book that fits easily in your pocket is what suits you, or perhaps you would rather use scraps of paper and old envelopes that are not bound and just collect these together in a box or file – it really doesn't matter. The important thing is to record all of these observations and ideas somewhere. You will need to be able to access them when required, so if you cannot rely on your memory, write on the box, or book, or file what is inside.

Over the years I have come to prefer an A5 landscape sketchbook filled with about a hundred sheets of Saunders Waterford cotton mould watercolour paper. Because I use my sketchbook almost exclusively to draw in I need a paper that is smooth enough for my dip pen to travel easily over but heavy enough for watercolour should I wish to add it. I rarely stick things into my sketchbook (I use scrapbooks for this) so I do not need pockets or to tear pages out to accommodate printed ephemera. I find the A5 landscape size big enough but not too obtrusive and having just the right sketchbook makes keeping it a pure pleasure.

If you are not used to keeping a sketchbook try starting off with a standard bound plain white paper sketchbook. It can help to treat the pages before you work on them, as white paper can be intimidating (some suggestions for this are given in Project Four: 'Preparing your Sketchbook'). There is a satisfaction in completing a sketchbook and starting a new one, so choose a book that has not too many pages. You will find it less daunting and once you have finished your sketchbook you can analyse what you did and did not like about it before buying or making another.

It sometimes helps to give your sketchbook a theme, for example a 'food' or 'dogs' sketchbook. I have never managed to keep this kind of book and always end up drawing everything and anything in mine but I do sometimes develop themed sketchbooks when working on a specific story. Keep your sketchbook with you all the time as you never know when you might need it, and try to use it every day. You are not keeping the sketchbook for anyone but yourself and no one but you need ever see it so do not worry what goes in it. It does not need to be neat or precious or filled with wonderful drawing; it is a place to explore, develop and investigate.

I have always greatly enjoyed drawing in zoos and whichever city I am in I always take the time to visit the zoo. I must have drawn in over forty zoos all over the world. Animals often appear in children's picture books so I am building up a store for future reference but I also love just drawing animals. They are a challenge as they constantly move. Even when they are still one never knows when they might start moving again so there is great urgency to the drawing, one must get down what one can as quickly as possible. Because the animals are moving it is probable that many of the drawings I start I will be unable to finish; therefore I often end up with pages of eyes or heads. Sometimes the animal will return to this position so I can add to the drawing, in which case I will draw over the previous drawings if necessary, sometimes not. A fairly large sketchbook is useful here because I need to see as many of my drawings as possible so that if the opportunity arises I can add to it. I cannot be flicking through my sketchbook looking for a particular drawing because by the time I have found it the animal will probably have moved. Besides, this interrupts the concentration, which needs to be intense when drawing animals. A fountain pen is particularly useful for drawing animals because one cannot fiddle about with this subject matter. This needs confidence and a pen mark does not offer the opportunity for rubbing out so one might as well accept that many of the drawings will be no more than meaningless lines. What you are unlikely to get is one finished drawing of a lion. This is fine. What does tend to happen is that the more one draws a particular animal the better one gets at capturing its image. One gets to know what it really looks like and therefore the drawings become more meaningful. It is a good idea to stick with one type of animal for an hour or so at least. It is always useful to have colour with you at the zoo but do not feel obliged to use it. Parrots or tropical birds demand colour and with some of the animals, tigers, antelopes, it is useful in quickly putting down pattern or markings. Putting the colour in the correct place on something like a tiger absolutely transforms it. However, remember that what you are really after with zoo drawings is trying to capture something of the essence and character of the animal. These are things that one cannot capture from book reference or indeed from museum specimens. It can only be got from seeing and drawing the real thing.

These drawings of parrots were made at the Natural History Museum in Siena, Italy. Obviously, they were not going to move so there was the opportunity to add colour with care and at leisure. However, as I was the only guest in the museum, the lights, which were on a time switch, kept switching off and plunging me into complete darkness – the sensor not registering my stillness in standing drawing.

DRAWING FROM OBSERVATION

Of course it is one thing to be inspired by reading about keeping sketchbooks. You have been to the library and looked at printed artists' sketchbooks. You have been online and turned the pages of illustrators' sketchbooks. You have bought or made yourself a beautiful sketchbook. You have your pencils sharpened, your fountain pen filled. Now what to draw? This is the moment where many sketchbooks die. What exactly shall I draw? The answer: just draw something.

One can never know what might prove useful in the future so try to draw everything that you are interested in. If you are interested in your subject you will probably produce a better drawing; you will certainly enjoy it more. Drawing directly from observation is excellent practice. Investigating, through drawing how something works or is put together, drawing from a variety of angles and viewpoints the same object, making drawings of the same thing using a series of different media – all of these make great starting points. When it comes to working on your story this kind of back-up material will be invaluable.

DRAWING ON LOCATION

Going out on location to draw the things in your book cannot fail to make better illustrations. When one is working on a children's book, or any book come to that, it is essential to have a

In these stunning location drawings over the last four pages: Bovril advertisement (page 26); Columbia Road, Electric Avenue (page 27); Regent's Canal, Michelin Building (page 28); Music Temple (right), by the reportage artist and illustrator James Oses we can see how he uses colour and line to capture the essence and atmosphere of these places. He uses the pen line with great confidence and this helps give these drawings life and energy.

knowledge of exactly how the people, places, and things in your story look so that you can draw them in a way that not only convinces but also communicates something of the atmosphere and qualities they possess. Clearly if you wait until you have written a story and then search around to draw from life all of the things in it you are in for a very long project. The trick is to constantly 'keep' a sketchbook so that when one is after a drawing of a specific object there is the possibility that one has previously drawn and recorded it. Obviously the longer and

more assiduously one keeps sketchbooks, the more likely this is to be the case.

It is often the case that many of the best ideas for stories occur whilst one is drawing on location. Something might happen, or one might overhear a phrase or conversation that sparks an idea. Once whilst drawing at a zoo I overheard two women talking about how an elderly relative had come from a family where all of the boys in the family had been given animal names – Robin, Leo, Peregrine, and so on. I thought this was a funny and

PROFILE: JAMES OSES

The illustrator and reportage artist James Oses makes a career of drawing on location.

I nearly always begin a project by going out to draw on location; for example, if the book is about penguins I might spend a day or two at the zoo drawing every conceivable type of penguin, discovering what they really look like, how they move, looking for character in their mannerisms. I am also looking for ideas, as one of the things when drawing on location is the unexpected – you never know what will happen.

I have a small sketchbook with me most of the time, which I can draw in anywhere, but I prefer individual sheets of paper. I take a sturdy piece of mount board with a couple of crocodile clips. I am quite fussy about paper and use Fabriano HP [hot press] 300g but obviously the paper depends on the medium you are using. I also carry an A4 landscape sketchbook.

I work mainly in pen. Pen is an unforgiving medium and when you make a line it is either right or wrong – there is no rubbing out – but this is what I like about it. If I am using colour I like to work by putting this in first, blocking it in with watercolour or crayons, then I draw over that. This keeps the pen as the main ingredient, the one dominant thing because it is going over the top. Colour is important. So much of what is around is about colour and I would lose a lot by not using it. I used to work almost totally in pen, working on the drawing to such an extent that there would be no room for the colour, so now I start with it.

It is very easy to get cold when drawing, it is always colder than I think it will be and if I am constantly thinking how cold I am then it makes it

James Oses.

hard to concentrate and I will want to go home. I am used to drawing in public so I no longer think anything of people looking or wanting to talk. I am flattered that people are interested and, after all, you never know whom you are talking to. The weather is far more difficult.

When I visit a museum I try to have a rough idea of what I want to draw before I go and nearly always stick to one room. Once I am in front of what I want to draw I try to make the most of it and record as much as possible.

I continually find inspiration by looking at illustrators like Ronald Searle, David Gentleman and Matthew Cook, masters of drawing on location. Paul Hogarth made a very successful and versatile career out of reportage; I cannot think of anything better.

perfect starting point to a story; maybe the girls were all flowers – Ivy, Rose, Daisy.

There is an enormous difference between drawing, let's say, a camel from a photograph and a camel directly from observation at the zoo. Photographs are better used as a last resort as they do not inspire and fire the imagination, as does the real thing. However, drawing on location is hard.

Take everything you might need: a small folding stool if you feel you may want to sit down (you need to be in a position to draw what you want from the most appropriate place, not what can be seen from a nearby bench). When you stay still for a long time it is easy to get cold; likewise if you are in strong sunlight take a hat.

An illustrator out drawing is an interesting thing, it would seem, to everyone. It is best to accept this and answer any questions with good humour, despite the distraction, rather than get cross. You will not produce good drawings if you allow yourself to become irritable and bad tempered.

When drawing on location one is primarily recording information that one may want to use back in the studio. Keep this fixed in your mind one is not producing a finished image to go in a book. You may find it helpful to tackle your subject along the following lines:

- Make a drawing of the whole thing.
- Where there are repetitions (for example, identical windows or doors), make one detailed study and indicate on a quick plan where these details occur.
- Make some colour notes either with colour or written notes, likening the colour to something you already know.
- Make written notes of noises or smells, or what you overhear; these may trigger the imagination later.
- If the location is busy draw the people in.
- Make several drawings around your subject, making sure to draw it from different viewpoints.
- Make a plan or diagram showing where everything goes.
- Try to make a drawing that captures something of the atmosphere.
- Try not to rub out in your sketchbook; either draw over or turn the page. Everything might be useful when you are back in your studio.
- Take a photograph of the subject before you leave.

As you begin to use your sketchbooks, working from these drawings to create scenarios and pictures for your stories, you will come to know what it is about them that you find most useful and can make a point of seeking out this type of material to draw in future.

PROJECT FOUR: PREPARING YOUR SKETCHBOOK

It can be daunting to begin a sketchbook filled with pristine white paper; one does not want to feel inhibited or that one must draw well or else the book is spoilt. A good way to lessen the constraint of this is to prepare the pages in a variety of ways before you use the sketchbook. Treat the book as a series of double pages so when putting down a surface, cover both pages going across the middle of the book. Sketchbooks always work better treated in this way, whether preparing pages or just drawing in them. The rather too contrived method of drawing only on the right hand pages of a sketchbook, presumably in case you want to tear out a drawing, makes for a much less lively and exciting sketchbook. Put down several double page spreads of each surface then you can explore how different tools work on different surfaces. Anything goes, so be creative, but here are a few surfaces to try:

- White emulsion paint.
- Coffee or tea stain.
- Old packaging, recycled envelopes lightly painted over with white.
- Sepia ink or watercolour wash.
- Gum strip.
- Scotch magic tape.
- Patches of colour.
- Masking tape.
- PVA with water and mixed with a small amount of sugar or sand (a slightly gritty surface is what is required here).
- Graph or lined paper.
- Wallpaper.
- Brown paper.
- Watered-down Quink wash.
- Neutral coloured oil pastel.
- Printing ink applied with a roller, dry and sparingly.
- Newspapers, either text only or with images, or knocked back with a wash of white acrylic.

PROJECT FIVE:
SCRAPBOOKS

Scrapbooks are different from sketchbooks in that they are used to collect together printed ephemera. You can of course use your sketchbook for this purpose so that, as well as drawings, notes and visuals, your sketchbook also becomes a store for the useful printed imagery that you collect. The slight disadvantage with using your sketchbook in this way is that, unless one gets into the habit of tearing a page out each time one adds a ticket

or postcard, in order to accommodate the extra thickness, one ends up with a fat and distorted book, or even worse a broken spine. Also, if one is buying a sketchbook filled with a particular quality paper, because one likes working on it, it seems rather a shame to then tear half of it out.

If you are using a purpose-made scrapbook it should have spacers – strips of paper bound into the book between each double spread – to allow for the paper you are going to add when sticking things in. If you are making your own scrapbook

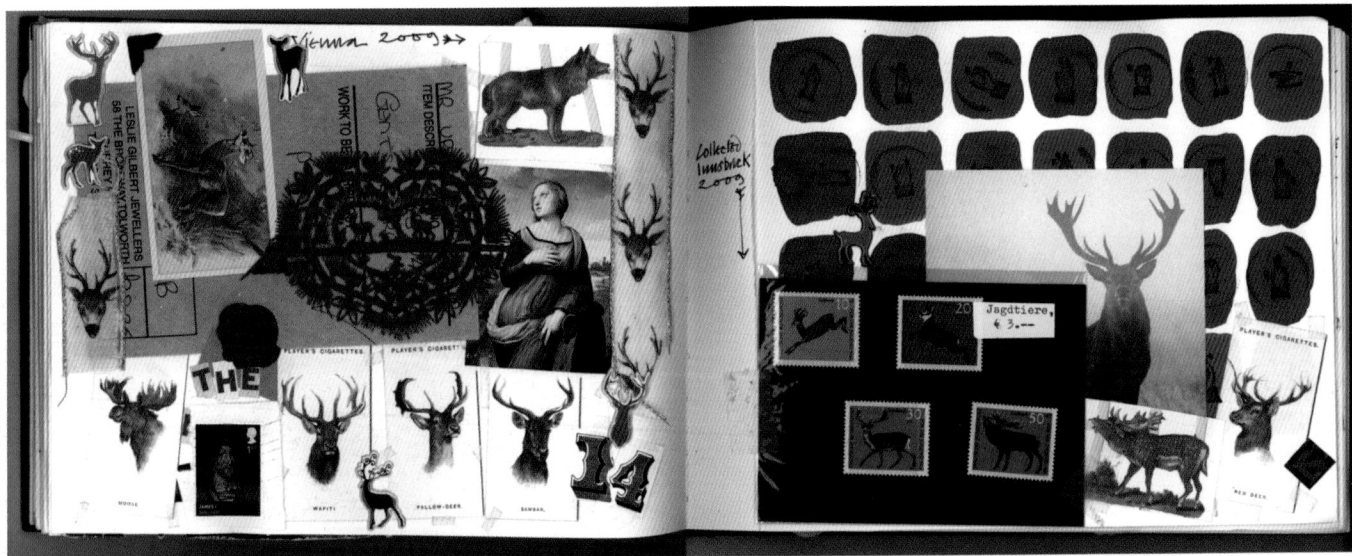

Scrap Book Three by Martin Ursell. These pages from one of my own scrapbooks are filled with various pieces of printed ephemera – tickets, tags, seed packets, collage material – anything and everything. I have a large box that I keep in the corner of my studio, which gradually fills with 'stuff' that I have collected. When time permits I assemble this stuff into scrapbooks. I do think about how this

then either accommodate this when binding or clipping the pages together, or adapt a book by tearing every alternate page out, using a ruler pressed into the spine so that the pages are torn from the book leaving 2cm or so, the width of the ruler, of the torn page in. This will prevent the pages falling out, but remember when sticking things in the book not to encroach on this middle area or you will still be adding to the thickness of the book.

Scrapbooks can be inspiring and a great trigger for the imag-

ination and it is well worth seeking out the available printed editions of artists and illustrators who have published their scrapbooks. *Scrapbooks: An American History* by Jessica Helfand and *Beaton: the Art of the Scrapbook*, by James Danziger, both make for inspiring browsing.

material is arranged on the page but not overly so; the important thing is to collect it all together in a form that I can easily access. I am lucky in having a good memory, so I can usually remember what I have in each book. However, it would probably be a wise idea to provide some sort of index for these books. Like all of such tasks, this would be much simpler to do as an ongoing activity.

Here is a double page of sketchbook thumbnails for the Book of Genesis. These roughs are drawn straight from my head without any reference. These roughs will change and evolve many times before they get to artwork.

In the beginning GOD created the heavens and the earth.

The earth was vast waste, darkness covered the deep, and the spirit of GOD hovered over the water. GOD said, 'LET THERE BE LIGHT' and there was light;

NIGHT

Chapter Three
STARTING A BOOK

So evening came and morning came; it was the FIRST DAY.

AND God saw that light was good, and he separated light from darkness.

He called the light DAY and the darkness NIGHT

It might seem an obvious point, but one of the first things to decide before starting a book is where you are going to work. Undertaking a project like writing and illustrating a picture book is a lengthy task that will almost certainly take up weeks or months and in some cases years of your time. One could work on the dining room table but then it will constantly be a case of clearing everything away and never being able to leave anything out. This discourages returning to work for odd moments of time and is far from ideal – although, of course, there must be many picture books that were created in just these surroundings.

If you have the possibility to create a space of your own to work in then this is by far the best course of action. Most illus-trators will have a studio where they can work undisturbed and where they can leave everything out to work on at any given moment. A studio needs good natural light but not blinding sunlight so position your desk near a suitable window. Take into account whether you are left handed or right handed and arrange your drawing board accordingly. You do not want the light from the window to make you have to work in the shadow of your hand.

Working at a drawing board all day can be a great strain on your eyes and it is very advantageous to be able to glance out of a window at a long view at regular intervals. This keeps your eyes exercised and over years of work is extremely effective in staving off damage by constantly focusing on a point just 12 inches or so from you.

At least two Anglepoise lights above and to the side of your drawing board will help when daylight is poor or fading. Many illustrators find it impossible to work in colour in artificial light because the colours can appear altered when viewed again in natural light. A good way of combating this is to have your Anglepoise on all the time so that the passing of day into dusk then night goes unnoticed. There are daylight bulbs available now which make working in colour at night much easier.

It is worth getting a good chair. Sitting at a drawing board even for relatively short periods of time can cause back problems, so sit properly and comfortably. A hump is as common a feature of illustrators as a callus on the index finger so making sure you have a good working environment can only add to your ability to produce good work.

Kitting your studio out is also worth consideration, as having plenty of your chosen media and materials leaves you with less

Clare Beaton's studio. Clare works with fabrics and textiles and her studio is dominated by a set of outfitter's drawers. Her desk is positioned in a bay window ensuring good light. Clare's cottons and materials are all within easy reach.

Martin Ursell's studio. I have a worktop running around the studio but choose to work underneath a skylight. The plan chest and small set of drawers are useful for nibs, paints and other materials. I am tidy so everything has its place.

to be concerned about. Layout paper for working on ideas and visuals is especially important, as is a box of pencils and something with which to keep them sharp. A light box, which is used to trace off ideas and drawings, is not essential by any means – one can achieve the same effect by holding a drawing up to the window – but it is a very useful piece of equipment, perhaps worth adding to your studio when money permits. Likewise a cutting mat and scalpel make the business of cutting and pasting images together very easy. Constructing a successful composition by assembling parts of different roughs together can save much time, so again, although not essential, a cutting mat and scalpel do earn their place in the studio.

Being able to stick up images that inspire or pieces of reference that you may wish to work from is also advantageous, so a pin board or wall space set aside for this purpose is very useful. Keep a box or drawer for scrap paper and find a place for old drawings; try not to throw drawings away, even those you think have gone badly. Seen again after a time, they can be viewed afresh and often seem much improved. It is good practice to hang on to all drawings until the end of a project, as you never know what might prove useful at a later date.

Finally, for many illustrators the minor distraction of some sort of background noise really is essential. This is obviously very much a matter of personal preference but some kind of unobtrusive background noise can help to keep the mind focused and attentive where complete silence can encourage daydreaming.

ROUGHS

Assuming you now have an idea to work with and a place to work in, the next thing is to begin by working on the roughs. 'Roughs' or 'visuals' are exactly that: often very rough drawings and sketches of how you think the illustrations might look. Roughs should initially be drawn straight from your head. You do not need to worry about reference or how recognizable the things you are trying to draw in your roughs book; what is important is that you try to communicate with your roughs what is going on in your story. Here you should consider scale and viewpoint, the relationship between the characters, composition, and what is going on in your story. Try alternative viewpoints and variations. Do not just settle for the first thing that pops into your head but draw it all down in your roughs again and again until you have explored every conceivable way of telling your story through drawing.

Keeping the scale of these roughs fairly small at first means that you will be less inclined to worry about the drawing and accuracy of the things you are trying to depict. It will also be quicker to produce more ideas if the roughs are small and you are more likely to be happy to explore and doodle, playing around with the possible ways of creating an image.

These small roughs and visuals will eventually evolve into a full-size dummy book but, at this early stage, before we have fed in our reference and worried about where the text will go, it is just a case of getting down in the quickest way possible all the variations that your imagination can conjure up.

A layout pad is ideal for this process. The paper is relatively cheap but great to draw on. The paper is translucent so it is possible to see through it and trace off it, or develop images that look promising. Layout paper can take wet materials and markers so adding colour is possible. It can also stand much overdrawing. Pencil is particularly good on layout paper and looks great when later enlarged on a photocopier.

Il Sung Na's Studio. In these two different images of Il Sung Na's studio we can see the two different sides of his work: the clean, ordered desk dominated by computers and technology, and the creative clutter of media, materials and visuals papering the wall space.

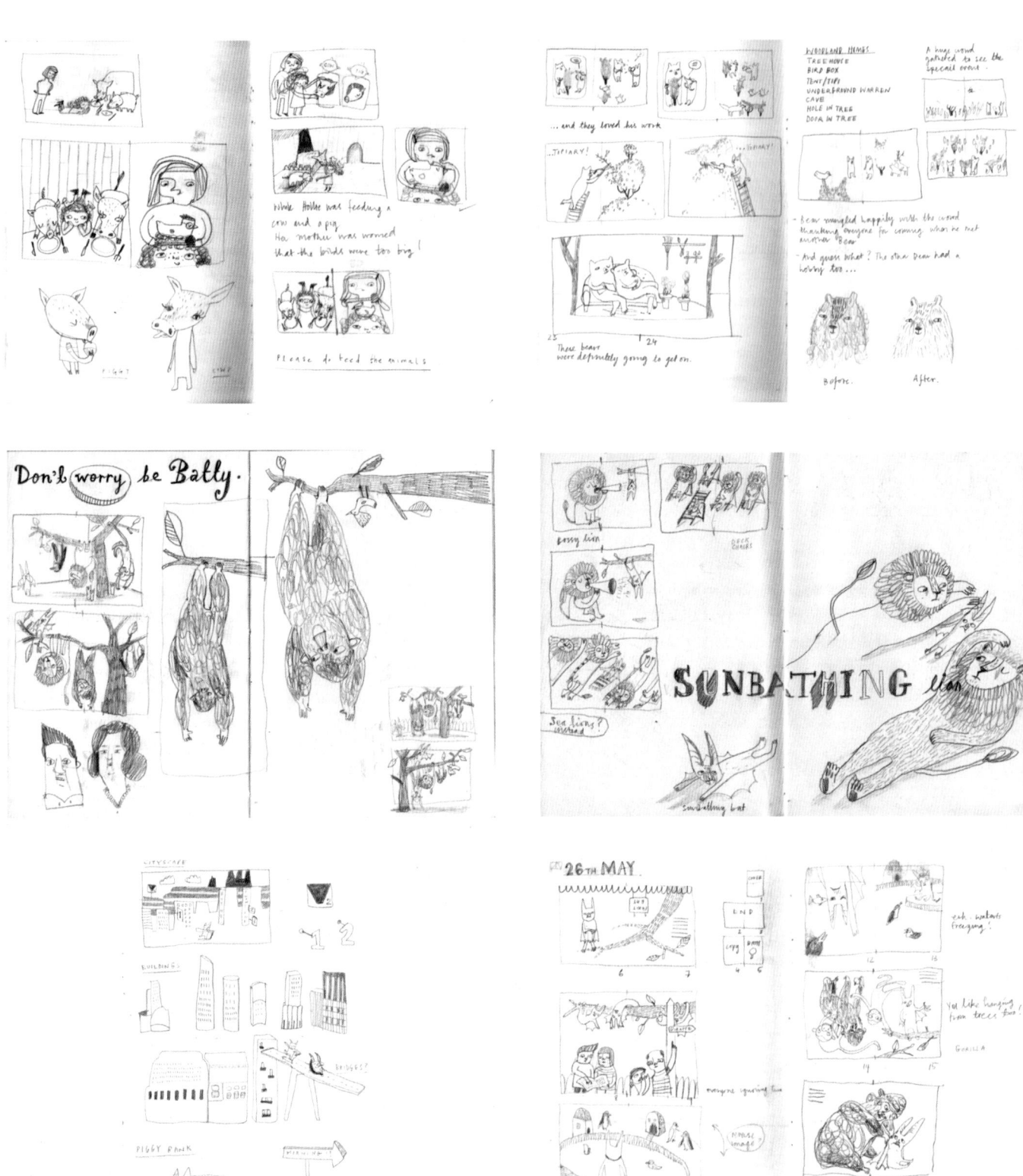

In these lively and fresh pencil drawings from Sarah Dyer's sketchbooks you can see how she is exploring various possibilities through roughs and visuals. Even at this early stage Sarah is thinking how these drawings might relate to the page. Also Sarah is playing with phrases and snatches of text; the story might very well emerge in this way. There are notes on reference (woodland homes), and character studies – everything is being considered and developed at the same time.

These pencil roughs are from a book I illustrated called *Dragon Boy* by Pippa Goodhart. I am exploring different ways of illustrating a part of the story where Dragon Boy discovers how to make fire, and this attracts his dragon friends. The two other roughs here are from earlier in the story when the 'fire-snatcher' steals some fire from the dragons. Both of these episodes are very exciting parts of the book.

Either draw the page outline first so that one may consider the composition, or cut out a window from another piece of paper proportionally to the correct size and move this across your image, again to enable you to arrive at a strong composition. One is assuming here that in both these cases the page outline is a rough guide. These are roughs; we are not using a ruler or measuring anything but if we are imagining our final page size will be portrait then we should be producing roughs to a portrait shape. Always draw the middle of the page in, and, if the illustrations are to appear as part of a double spread, always produce the roughs as double spreads. We need to see the roughs, however rough they may be, in the context of what else we will be seeing it against. In any kind of picture book one almost never works in single pages (this will be discussed in much greater depth in Chapter 5).

Sometimes when working on these early ideas for picture books it is useful to work in small 'concertinas', strips of paper that have been folded back and forth. The reason these concertinas are so useful is that one has the option of seeing the drawings as individual images or as a sequence – very useful when beginning to work out how to tell a story visually.

PROJECT SEVEN:
AESOP'S FABLE CONCERTINA

Aesop's fables provide a great source of workable material for creating stories. They are usually short and succinct, have incident and a moral at the end, which gives the whole thing a purpose.

Having chosen a story, read through it, breaking it into small paragraphs. Each one of these small paragraphs will be a different page and therefore a different illustration. You may wish to subdivide these paragraphs into sentences or even single words if you feel it would add to the telling of the story, perhaps rendering some of the text as speech, in speech bubbles, for example.

Now take a piece of cartridge paper and fold it in half, then back on itself and again, and so on until you have a concertina with the number of pages you require. Remember you will also need a cover and you could have a title page.

Drawing straight into the concertina, visualize your story, either writing in the text by hand or typesetting it on the computer and sticking it in. This is a very simple way of creating a picture book.

PROJECT EIGHT:
A STORY FROM A STORY

Visit a charity or secondhand bookshop and buy yourself a very cheap book (fiction or non-fiction – it really does not matter). Now look at the first page of text and delete or circle a series of words so that you create a new story, completely changing the meaning of the original text. When illustrating this you could copy the new story out and make a brand new book or you could illustrate directly in the book itself, making the obliterated text part of the illustration.

PROFILE: SARAH DYER

Sarah Dyer works as a successful picture book illustrator. Her many picture books include *Five Little Fiends*, which won the Smarties Book award.

Sarah Dyer.

Starting a book for me usually begins with wanting to draw a particular animal, creature or situation. I might then develop a character in my sketchbook. It is normally a fairly selfish reason, something I'd like to develop further because it inspires me to do so. If I sit and wait for an idea to come to me then that usually doesn't work. It is too forced and I get far too easily distracted by other things at my desk or on my computer. Sometimes an idea will stem from something overheard, often from a child, or a particular memory I have of my own childhood.

I usually begin with small drawings in my sketchbook. I love working in sketchbooks; I know that it is a very personal thing where people develop their ideas but for me a sketchbook works. It feels contained and safe. It also means that anything that I don't use remains for another day, like a catalogue or library of ideas. I then rough things out further, making small storyboards to explore pace, sequence and composition, all within my sketchbook. That is something I find invaluable, working out composition on a small scale. For some reason this works better, for me, than working full size. Almost always I end up using my tiny drawings and blowing them up full size and re-drawing them to keep the composition the same.

Keeping the early drawing basic also helps to maintain a charm and vitality in my final work. This is important, because in drawing them many times they can become stale. After I feel happy with the storyboarding in my sketchbook I will use these to make a first rough dummy book. It is important that I do not skip this stage of making the dummy book. Images look very different off a sheet of paper when put into a book. Page turning, left to right, edges of pages and page sequence all play a huge part in working out whether the narrative flows correctly.

An idea is normally worth pursuing if it continues to develop naturally, almost without really having to try. Many ideas that just don't have the mileage will sit in my sketchbooks waiting for something to happen to them, like a small, lost bunch of characters just waiting for the right story to come along! If I develop an idea and it naturally runs its course then I won't push it; there would be no point as I would only achieve a weak narrative and an equally weak set of drawings. I would also waste a lot of precious time.

Many of my ideas do not make it to a final book. This is no bad thing, however, as some turn into other stories, or are left out for good reasons. There is no point in shoe-horning something in just because I have become attached to it – I realize that more and more.

I find getting the text right one of the most difficult stages of making a picture book. Having a great idea is one thing but it can be very difficult to describe the story and fit it into just 32 pages. Another difficulty is moving to that final stage of decision-making: I am happy in my sketchbook but making any important decisions can be very hard. Sometimes I get unnecessarily attached to certain ideas or layouts. Working by myself does not help and I often need to show it to other people in order to judge if an idea is working or not. Sometimes you have to let an idea go even if you really, really, really don't want to!

I find I cannot just draw from my mind as my images are often weak and obvious. I find things

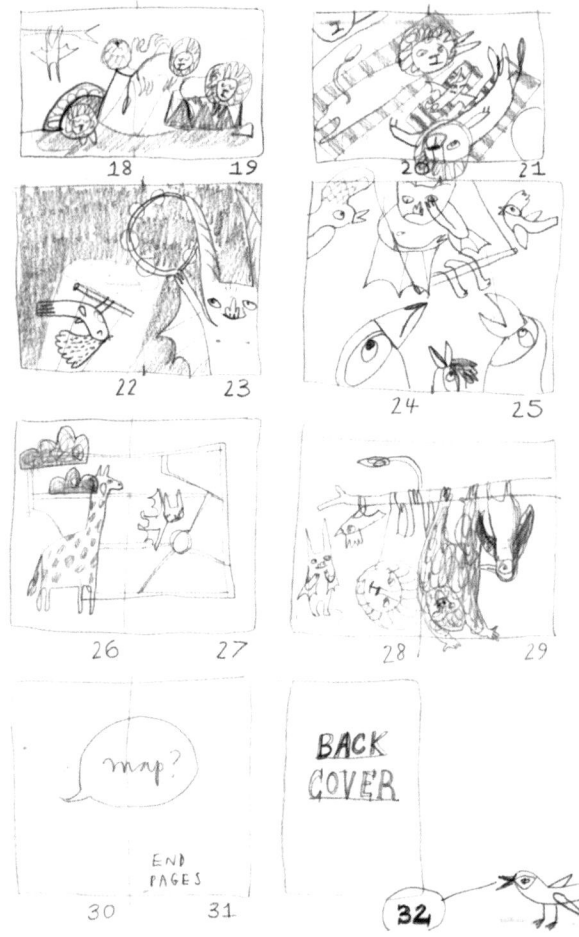

are far better if I either go out and look for what it is I want to draw, or at least find imagery that is relevant in books, or the Internet as a last resort. Everything I draw is referenced: buildings, clothing and composition are always better if I have interesting imagery to look at. I like getting the details just right. I would not be happy drawing a bird, for example, unless I knew what colour and kind of feathers it had; even if I then simplify this later, at least I knew at the beginning what they looked like.

Most of the time if I have got a picture book past the storyboard stage and on to a final dummy book I pretty much know it'll be OK. It doesn't really ever go 'wrong' at this stage. However, that doesn't mean it is safe from adjustments and final tweaks.

It is never really free from last-minute changes from the publishers anyway. I think you have to be very open to further changes even when you think it is perfect and couldn't possibly change. The

book may be mine at the beginning but as it goes along many people get involved with it and they all have an opinion on how it could be improved. This is part of the book-making process – it is not a bad thing, just part of the challenge of producing a children's book.

I have two favourite stages in making a picture book: the initial beginning, when exciting things are just developing and it is all new and I get to spend ages researching and drawing things I've been itching to draw; then I also really enjoy laying down the colour.

I am completely obsessed with Caran d'Ache Neocolor. They are glorious little oil pastel-like sticks of intensive colour; they lay down a flat colour so well. I love all colouring pencils especially the more waxy ones. My favourites were Karisma colour pencils but unfortunately the manufacturer stopped making them, much to my horror. Sometimes I think it is better to be open to

new media in case a project takes you in a new direction, work-wise. I like the idea of being open to this and not stuck in a rut of only ever working one way. Of course you have to have a trusting publisher for this to really work well.

It is sometimes difficult to imagine what children are looking for in a picture book. Children vary a lot from child to child and age to age. I do, however, think that most children enjoy humour, interesting image making, discovery and something that they can relate to. It is difficult to take yourself back to childhood and think what it was that engaged you. Most children know right from wrong but that doesn't mean they want a lesson in it.

I also think that children love images. I know as an illustrator that I am probably a little biased but I really think that a child's level of sophistication is so high. Visual language is very important to them; they understand and learn so much by looking and copying what is around them. I sometimes think that children prefer a book the more times they read it, so I like to include a lot of small details that they can discover read after read.

My own favourite illustrators are Beatrice Alemagna, Kveta Pacovská, Laura Carlin, Richard Scarry, the list goes on and on. I am inspired by their illustrations – their use of space and graphic language in telling a story. Saul Steinberg, Eric Ravilious, Charley Harper and many outsider artists also inspire me. I look to old illustrated animal and science biology books and Observer books for much of my reference.

PROJECT NINE:
THE LIFE AND DEATH OF …

This project is about telling a story from beginning to end with a sequence of images.

Either in a concertina or on a large sheet of paper, illustrate with a series of pictures the life and death of one of the following. Try to capture the drama and excitement with your chosen subject. Maybe there is an element of surprise or suspense. Parts of the sequence might call for a number of consecutive images; maybe you could use scale or pop-up elements to add to the interest. At the climax you might have a large fold-out page. The life and death of …

- a volcano
- a robbery
- a shipwreck
- a flea
- a letter
- a tree
- a pair of shoes
- a star
- a building
- a ghost

This double page rough entitled Plot 27 was originally created for a student magazine called *MEOW*. Having written and illustrated the story to fit in this space it occurred to me that it could work very well as a 32-page picture book, with some alterations to the characters and a little more 'fleshing out' of the story. Looking back at previous work or using and adapting earlier ideas are excellent starting points for new stories.

In these early character studies for Wesley Robins' book *A Fowl Journey*, his playful line and wonderful attention to detail enable one to see how these drawings are turning into real personalities. With these doodles Wesley is exploring the possibilities for beards, moustaches, costumes and hairstyles. How his characters might enjoy a drink is explored in little thumbnail sketches, and even the potential for surrounding paraphernalia, like a cake stand, is noted down and recorded for possible later use.

Chapter Four
DEVELOPING A CHARACTER

This is a difficult chapter to write because there are many different ways in which characters are developed and I think different approaches work for different illustrators. You may be basing your character on someone you know or perhaps a composite of several different people. Perhaps the character is completely imagined, or pure stereotype, or a mixture of all these things. Where on earth does one begin? Simply looking at what is around you and drawing it is a good starting point.

THE SKETCHBOOK AGAIN

As is so often the case, an excellent beginning is to go out with a sketchbook and draw directly from observation. If your character is a five-year-old boy, then draw five-year-old boys. If your character is a lion then go to the zoo and draw lions. Whatever it is, draw it from life. You will see how it moves, you will notice the proportion of things, and might observe characteristics or mannerisms.

Let us imagine that your character is a dragon or witch, however. It is not every day that one may set out with a sketchbook to draw one of these. With fictitious characters like this, go to the nearest available source, so for the dragon draw iguanas or lizards. Even if you end up with a dragon that bears little relation to these source drawings, the very experience of watching and drawing these creatures will repay you tenfold. Capturing something of the real thing in your illustration, the way it blinks or arranges its limbs, helps reinforce the veracity of your imagined character.

As noted previously, the living, breathing article is best but this can be backed up by museum studies or book reference where detail and in-depth study is required.

IDIOSYNCRASIES

Having researched your characters thoroughly through your sketchbook, one should be bursting with material to use. Creating a character is to do with observing how things behave and react to one another and, having noticed this, exaggerating it so that it becomes easily recognizable to everyone else. It is all about looking; that is why the sketchbook is so very important. The particular way in which someone walking on a windy, rainy day, with an umbrella, holds themselves and the umbrella is a difficult thing to make up. The strange thing is that although one may struggle to get this right without falling back on first-hand sketchbook reference, it is obvious to all when it is not quite right. Everyone notices that something is wrong even though they might not be able to say what is right. Exaggerating these observations only adds to the humour and wit of the illustration, helping the reader to acknowledge that this is just what it is like.

Therefore when developing a character, try to notice in your drawings what it is that you might be able to develop that is interesting. It might be the way they stand, or a particular care with their costume or exactly the opposite – complete carelessness with their costume. Really think about your character. Do they have glasses? If so what kind of glasses do they have? This

In these studies drawn on location, from one of Wesley Robins' sketchbooks, one can already see the potential for development in these people. Capturing directly from life the way people stand, what they wear and what they are doing is all invaluable reference material. One can see at a glance that to move from these observational drawings to Wesley's more imaginative character studies is not such a big leap.

These pages from Wesley Robins' sketchbook show clearly the development, and the thinking process, from observational studies through to imagined characters. In the final page of drawings we can see the individual characters really begin to emerge. Notice that Wesley does not begin to introduce colour until quite late in the process.

will make an enormous difference to how we perceive them. Everything will communicate something about your character: what they are wearing, the colour of it, how it is worn, the condition of it – the possibilities here are endless.

STEREOTYPES

There is a difference between using stereotypes and making generic illustration. Whereas with stereotypical characters one is exaggerating characteristics that communicate to the reader clearly the information one wants to convey, with a generic image one is falling back on a stylized way of drawing that communicates nothing but style. It is a good idea to avoid generic imagery and the best way to do this is, yet again, is to begin by drawing from life.

Stereotypes are useful, essential even, in communicating character. However, there is a subtlety to this, in other words a point where one can become too obvious and therefore produce a character that is dull and boring. For example, if your story calls for a witch, one immediately thinks of a warty, hooked nose, chin curving up to meet it, long hair, missing teeth; but one needs more than this if the witch is to have character, otherwise she is just a stereotypical witch without any character. How might one develop this? The thing to do is to go back to the story. Exactly what kind of witch is she? Is she a witch that likes nice things? Is she a witch that is kind but scatty? If she is kind and scatty then perhaps, as well as the stereotype details that convey witch, we can see that she has kind eyes or is holding her cat in a loving, gentle way and she has odd shoes on or a coat with the buttons done up wrongly. This is the essence of developing a character.

GETTING INTO CHARACTER

Thinking yourself into the mind of your character is another way of making them interesting when creating them. Imagining what they eat, what kind of cups or plates they eat from, the kind of chair they sit on – all of these things help realize the character. It is rather like the game where one imagines a friend as something else entirely. For example, if a particular friend were an animal, or a biscuit, exactly what type of animal or biscuit would they be?

When developing a character, create a world for them in your imagination and try to draw it. It might be that much of this background drawing is not included in the finished illustrations but the process will help you define them and so it is time well spent.

DRAWING THE SAME CHARACTER AGAIN AND AGAIN

When working on a picture book it is almost certain that you will need to draw your characters many times. The characters are going to be with you throughout the making of the story, and this will be over a period of time, maybe weeks or even months. They will be experiencing various emotions that you will want to show, and be engaging in lots of different activities. Whatever your character, we need to be able to recognize it each time it appears; it will be no good if we think it is a different character each time. This is hard to achieve: different emotions change the face. We know from experience that someone angry and shouting can look radically different from the same person asleep.

If your characters are wearing clothes then keeping them in the same outfits throughout the story is a great help. Never mind that the story may run the course of several days or longer, if you change their clothes then they will look different. If there is no avoiding this (for example, the character spends some time at night in bed but then goes out in the daytime), then look at giving your character other distinguishing features. Hairstyles, and hair colour are useful here.

Of course, the best advice is to draw your character so many times – happy, sad, crying, angry, shy, envious, interested, proud, embarrassed – that you can draw them inside out in any situation. This takes time, skill and a very great deal of practice but it is what being an illustrator is all about and this is at the root of developing a character.

These pages show the character development of various animals from Il Sung Na's *ZZzzz: A Book of Sleep, Brrr: A Book of Winter,* and *Hide and Seek*. Even at these very early stages one can see that Il Sung is thinking of how these characters will fit into a composition. One can also see that colour and decorative pattern play an important part in creating these animal characters. Even during these initial explorations Il Sung is experimenting with media, using everything and anything to create these beasts.

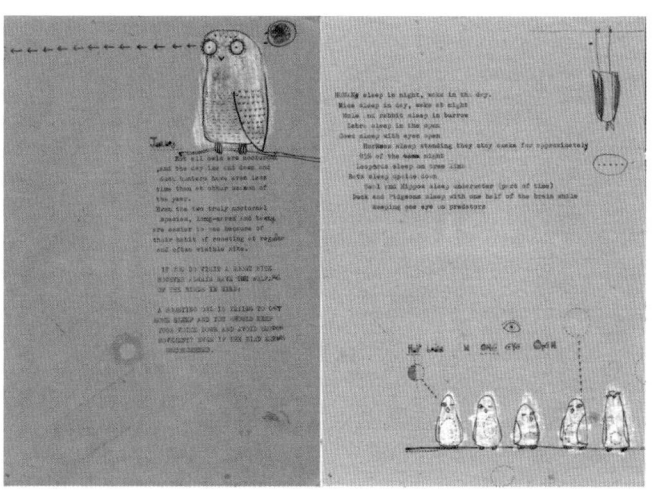

In these sketchbook pages I am developing the character of Cock Robin, who in this retelling of the old nursery rhyme is not a nice character at all. Starting with drawings made from a stuffed specimen I am trying to give him the appearance of the blackmailer he is by developing his features, particularly his eyes. The eyes are a very expressive feature and obviously his expression is key to helping us read what he is thinking. However, I am also exploring his posture with these drawings. Making him stoop, keeping his head low and giving him a slightly drooping wing are all adding to the idea that he is furtive and up to no good.

In the final image we see how Cock Robin appeared in the artwork: the culmination of sketchbook observational drawing, reference, ideas and character development all coming together. Starting with the original drawings of the stuffed robin has proved invaluable in creating a believable but animated character. There is never any substitute for drawing from the real thing.

ANIMAL CHARACTERS

When creating animal characters for stories there are many decisions to be made at the outset. To start with, how realistic does the animal need to be? There is a difference between a lion that might hunt and kill an antelope and a lion that might say, 'Good morning'.

Giving your animals the right kind of character for the story they are in is important. You have the option of whether or not they are wearing clothes. You may feel that they should walk on two legs, if they do not already. In fact reading the story carefully and noting down exactly what is required of them is essential. It may be a lion but perhaps in the story the lion needs to sit at a table or knit a jumper and these tasks will inevitably affect how you draw him.

Clothed or unclothed?

Dressing animals up in clothes has been very much out of fashion for probably thirty years or more. Even in books for very young children animals usually appear rendered in their natural skins. This is interesting because obviously the main determining factor in whether to dress up an animal or not will depend on what they have to do in the story.

I imagine this to be largely due to the changing attitude towards animals during the last third of the twentieth century. Zoos and animal parks are often seen as dubious places; despite the vanishing natural habitat of many species on earth most people think it unacceptable for animals to be kept in cages and maybe they are correct. Circuses with animals in are almost universally condemned, so perhaps it is not so surprising that our taste for dressing animals up has ebbed.

Of course there is a difference between animals in clothes and people with animal heads. In Kenneth Grahame's *The Wind in the Willows*, the characters Ratty, Badger, Mole and Toad are really people in all but name. They have picnics and drive cars, they row boats and live in human houses; it would be impossible to illustrate a book like this without dressing the animals. For one thing the clothes are referred to in the text but more than this, the adventures that these four animals get up to require hands. In Arthur Rackham's stunning illustrations for this book he has made the decision firstly to draw the characters as people with animal heads, although nevertheless he finds a way of bringing the essence of each creature into their costume: Mole wears a black fur suit; Badger is dressed in fusty tweeds. Secondly, he has needed to deal with the disparity in the scale of the characters. Toad swaps clothes with a human girl and Mole

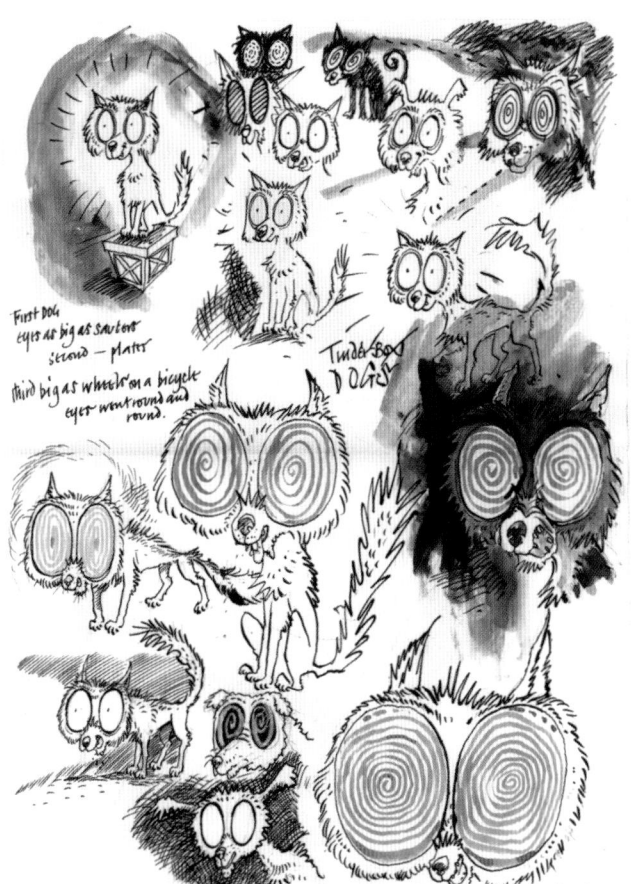

These drawings of mine show the final page in studies for the three dogs, with enormous eyes, from Hans Christian Andersen's *The Tinder Box*. By this stage I am thinking about colour and how to make each of the three dogs' eyes even more striking than the dog before.

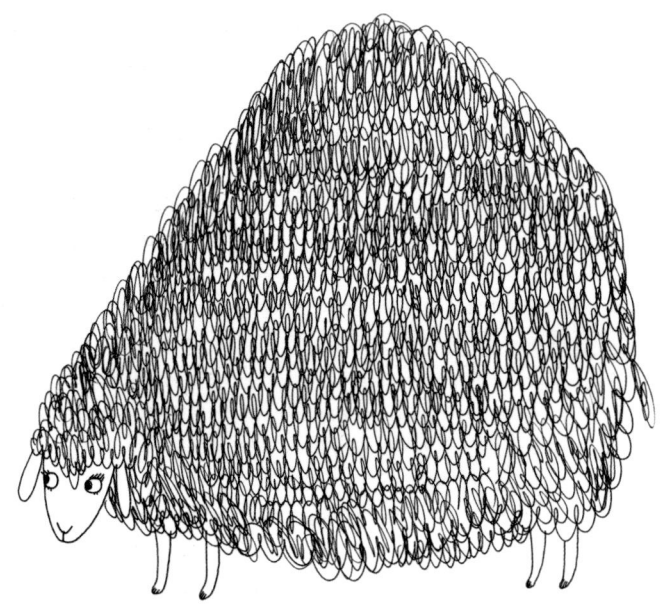

Sheep by Rina Donnersmarck.

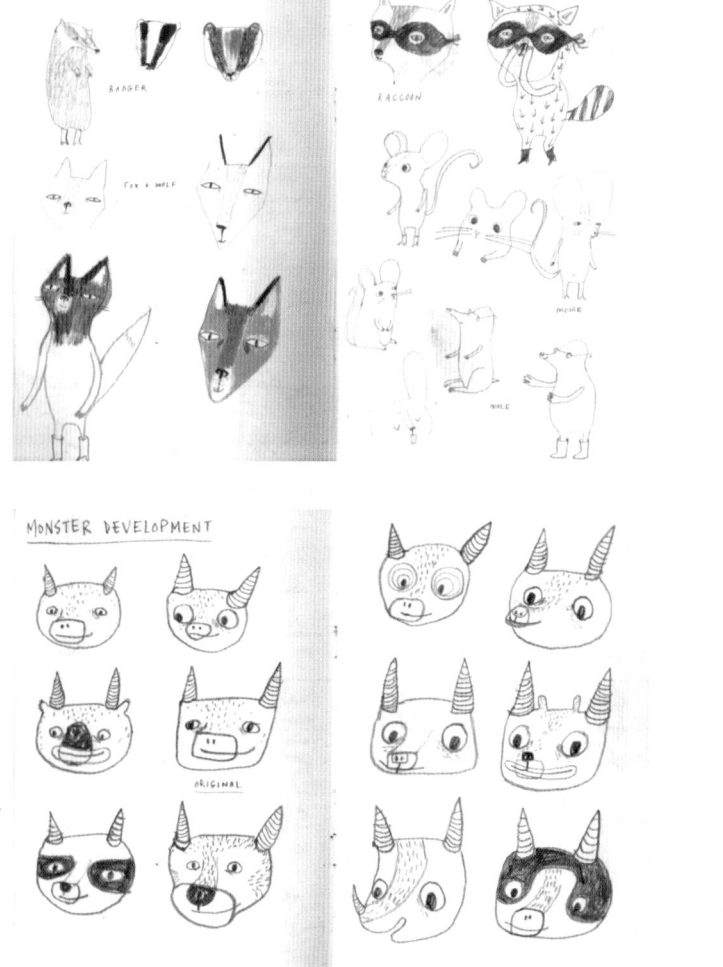

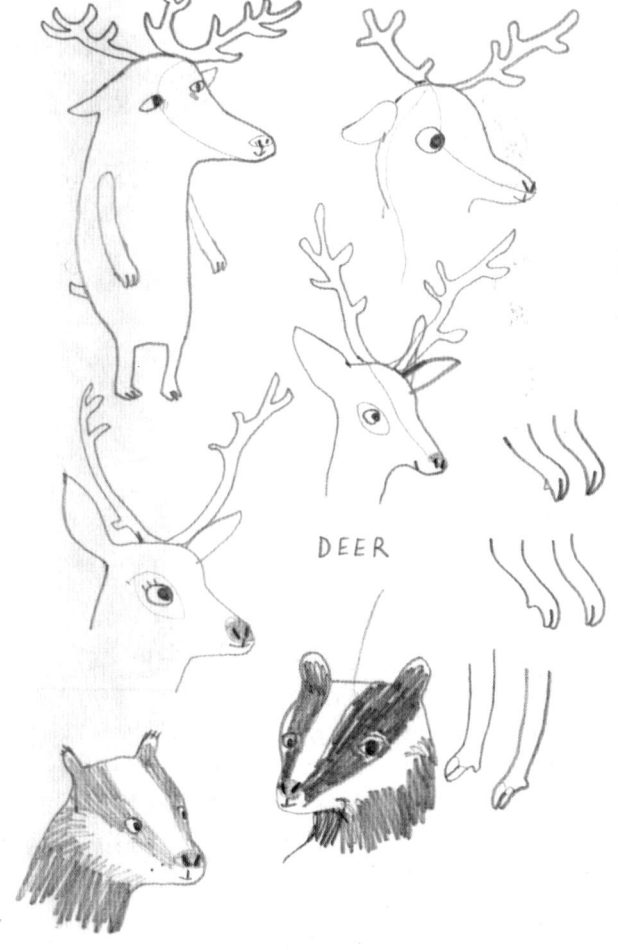

Character studies from Sarah Dyer's sketchbook.

sits at the table with Badger. Arthur Rackham does this so well that when we look at these beautiful illustrations we are hardly even aware of the dichotomy here.

There is a half-way stage that one might adopt, where the animal is basically represented as an animal but will wear one or two items of clothing. Beatrix Potter in the main opts for this approach. Her animals are always animals and she draws these supremely well but Peter Rabbit wears a blue coat in addition to his fur. Squirrel Nutkin wears nothing and although Samuel Whiskers wears the full works – a pea green jacket, dandy cream trousers and matching waistcoat with wonderfully pointy brown shoes – he is still in essence a rat, even with his human hands.

It is worth stressing again that when developing the characters for stories it is vital to take the time to carefully read the text so that you know what it is that they are required to do. The clues are here.

THE USE OF COLOUR

Remember when creating characters that you are able to consider everything: just because elephants are grey in real life does not mean they must be grey in your book. One could have an elephant blue or lilac, brown or sandy. These colours are near enough to grey and in the context of a story could almost pass without notice as within the realms of possibility. However, in your development sheets try every variation you can think of. Your elephant might be cerise, green or patterned floral. Many illustrators working in collage treat their animals in this way and it makes for lively and exciting illustration. The important thing is to let your imagination run wild on these initial character study sheets. Refining and editing away the more outlandish elements may need to come into play later but using your imagination at the beginning will almost certainly help you create more interesting and memorable characters.

THE WAY IN WHICH ONE DRAWS

The way in which one draws is of course a determining factor when creating a character. Many illustrators worry about 'getting' a style. In fact having taught on a variety of illustration courses over the years I would say that this was the most common worry of would-be illustrators, not having a style and how to get one. This is a nonsense.

One's 'style' is simply the way one draws. Just as we all write in a distinctive way, drawing is no different. How one draws, like how one writes, is affected by a variety of things. The media one uses is the most obvious. Drawing with a stick of charcoal as opposed to a fine liner pen will give the drawing a very different feel. Keep this in mind when you are creating your characters and try to explore drawing with a varied and diverse set of materials.

Our influences and those we admire might also affect the way we draw. Hopefully this will be something we are just influenced by; looking at how others use media and make images is to be encouraged and it is one of the ways we learn. Taking this knowledge and developing it in our way, not slavishly copying or imitating someone else's way of working, is essential. It can be difficult to avoid the trap of copying a favourite illustrator's style. The solution yet again is to go back to drawing directly from observation. It is here that the real character of your drawing burns through.

As a final suggestion one may try drawing with one's 'second' hand. If you are right-handed try drawing with your left. This might give your illustrations a quirky, untamed look but it will certainly help keep the line exciting and full of life. The point is, when creating and developing characters, try everything; it can only help and you may stumble upon something wonderful.

PROJECT TEN:
PINK ELEPHANTS

A very simple exercise that is very useful for opening up the imagination is to try rendering animal characters in a variety of colours and patterns.

Make a drawing of an animal character. Now reproduce this same drawing twenty or so times. Reproduce the drawing in exactly the same way each time – photocopies or printouts from the computer are excellent. Do not be tempted to try different angles or positions with your character at this point. The object of this exercise is to see the impact of different treatments on your character so for this the character needs to be identical each time.

Now render these character drawings in a variety of colours, patterns, materials and effects. Really try to be as imaginative and as open as you can and try everything: you might be surprised at the results.

PROJECT ELEVEN:
CHARACTER SKETCHBOOK

Taking yourself out for a few hours with a sketchbook is always a good idea. Decide firstly what kind of character you wish to draw. Keep it fairly broad – children, old ladies, people with dogs, people at work, cyclists, that kind of thing – and find a suitable place from which to draw. You will have already edited

PROFILE: WESLEY ROBINS

Illustrator Wesley Robins won the Macmillan Children's Book Prize in 2008 for his book *A Fowl Journey*. The book features an extraordinary range of characters.

My characters are a mix of observational drawings and imagination. I like talking to people, those that are memorable that is, and 'nick' their various characteristics in drawing. These are real people in my illustrations and usually, when I am drawing them, these people come up and so a conversation begins.

I find I get the best ideas for characters from real life. Weird names, reading people's experiences and anecdotes are all potential starting points for stories and characters. I keep little notebooks of themes and story threads. I draw in them and write down ideas. I doodle and scribble in them and somehow, out of all of this the characters evolve. I think using stereotypical imagery is important because my readers will want to recognize what type of character I have drawn. If I drew a tracksuited explorer, people would wonder where the moustache and explorer's hat were ... I would wonder where the moustache and explorer's hat were. What makes characters interesting is spotting these qualities; one does not want this to become predictable, but likewise communicating effectively will inevitably require characteristics that people can recognize.

With all of my characters I am imagining the world from which they all come. The scale might change but I am always very interested in what they are wearing. I like the regalia and details of my characters. Gowns, ceremony and pomp are great fun to draw, using colour and therefore hopefully adding atmosphere to the things I am drawing. I love producing pages of little characters, battle scenes, panoramas. I do like history and this nearly always plays a part in my illustrations.

I like to use smooth paper and draw on this with a fine liner, a 0.05 or 0.1, always black ink. I use all sorts for colour but nothing that will obscure my line, so watercolours, inks. I introduce texture with photoshop. I like particular blues – Prussian blue is an personal favourite. I am a big sketchbook worker and like to make my own sketchbooks, stitching them together with various types of paper, usually whatever is cheap!

In the sketchbooks I begin starting a story by developing characters, small pages of ideas; there are no constraints at the beginning. By the time I get to the artwork I have it fixed in my head exactly how it should look but it can still go wrong for me at the artwork stage. I am constantly refining and changing my illustrations, working things over and over again and I think it is good to exhaust every possibility. Time constraints and deadlines make the final choice necessary but I am never totally happy with anything!

Although I was always constantly drawing as a child I never really considered illustration as a career. I went with a friend who was interested in doing a foundation course and thought I would quite like it, so I joined. This worked and an illustration degree and the rest followed. Winning the Macmillan children's book prize was exciting and opened lots of doors. It was a huge boost to my confidence and looks great on my CV, and it was a great way of making contacts right at the beginning of my career.

I find I am inspired by lots of different illustrators but I am not great with names; John McNaught and Quentin Blake are two I can always remember, real favourites.

Wesley Robins.

possible subject matter by choosing your category so think where would be the best place to go. To draw people with dogs a park would be ideal but for old ladies a bus might be better. When you have a collection of drawings try to analyse what you have with further drawings. For example, with your 'old ladies' sketchbook, look at their footwear or the type of bag they might have. You can extend this by noticing details about your chosen subject whenever the opportunity occurs.

A series of books on different themes built up in this way forms an invaluable store of reference.

PROJECT TWELVE:
BUILDING ON A STEREOTYPE

Make a list of a series of characters that you might want to include in a story – for example a trendy aunt, a bully, a know-all, a shy child, someone wise, etc. Now write down everything that you could draw in order to communicate your character, the stereotypical details in other words.

Create your stereotype bully or whatever it is you have decided upon.

Now, using this character drawing as a starting point, give him different character traits. It is easy enough to imagine him as a dandy bully, or a scruffy bully, but slightly more difficult would be an old man bully or a thin bully. How does one convey the character of a bully – is it in the hairstyle or the posture (the angle of the head and hands), or is it in the eyes?

Try developing this on to an animal, a bully dog or cat. A bully lion or tiger are relatively easy to create but a bully rabbit or bear cub are more difficult. Are you finding that there is one element that needs to be included each time for the character of a bully to be successfully communicated?

PROJECT THIRTEEN:
SAME CHARACTER, DIFFERENT EXPRESSIONS

Getting the expressions of your character right so that they communicate the emotion that you intend is essential. The character you have created is really no different to an actor and we would give short shrift to an actor whose face never changed or looked frightened when they should be looking surprised.

Choose a character that you have developed and are comfortable with drawing. Give him as many different expressions as you can think of (the list below offers a starting point). Look in the mirror at your own facial expressions to get them exactly right. There is really no substitute for this.

To test out how successful you have been, try your characters on other people and hope they reply with the expression that you intended.

- Sceptical
- Amused
- Impatient
- Ashamed
- Surprised
- Tired
- Worried
- Frightened
- Full of contempt
- Sly
- Amazed

Here are the beginnings of a dummy book. The story, called *Wenceslas*, is mapped out here as double page spreads. The text is hand written alongside the image so that there will be no danger of forgetting to leave enough room for it, and thought is being given to the effect of the 'gutter' (where the pages meet) on the illustration. This small paper dummy book will be the first in maybe two or three versions, each gradually increasing in size and detail. The final version of this small book I mailed out as a Christmas 'card', something I do every year.

Wenceslas was probably born around 907. His father died when he was nine years old and his cruel and ruthless mother ruled over the Kingdom of Bohemia.

④

⑤

The Queen had no t... for Wenceslas and sent him to live with his grandmother the old Queen Ludmilla. His younger brother Boleslav she kept with her.

⑧

⑨

Chapter Five
THE DUMMY BOOK

Queen Lu... she had killed.

⑬

Wenceslas rode out to meet him and was surrounded by Boleslav and his men who hacked him to pieces.

Boleslav became King. Legend has that not a single drop of blood flowed from Wenceslas' wounds. Wenceslas w... twenty two wh... he was murder... He was canoni... and became pat...

Three picture book dummies (from left): *Three Kings* by Martin Ursell; *The Witch's Dog* by Carolyn Dinan;
Who Really Killed Cock Robin? by Martin Ursell.

Because of the way books are printed, nearly all children's picture books are 32 pages long. There are various ways of using these pages but if you always work to a 32-page format you will save yourself much trouble when looking to find a publisher for your book.

Take an A4 sheet of paper and fold it in half three times so that you make a little book. Now hold it so that the folded corner is top left (see page 72). Number the pages and this will start with page 1 and end with page 16; pages 8 and 9 will be in the middle of your 'little book'. If you now open out the sheet of paper you will see immediately that all of the numbers are jumbled up but that pages eight and nine, the middle spread, remain next to each other. This is called a natural double spread. A 32-page picture book will contain two of these folded sheets of paper and will therefore have two of these natural doubles. This is important because when illustrating for a picture book any image that crosses the middle of a double page spread runs the risk of being distorted or cropped when the book is bound but on a natural double the impact of this is much less.

It is also worth noting at this point that picture books are usually made up of these 16-page sections. As has been said, 32 pages is almost always the length of a children's picture book but 48-page books and then 64-page books are alternatives for longer books.

As with all generalizations, there are exceptions: 24-page books are quite possible. It is possible to add fewer than 16 pages when wanting to increase the size of a book. Books where paper engineering, or pop-up books are a factor also do not follow these general rules. However, it is perfectly valid to take the 16-page section and therefore the 32-page children's picture book as the most used and most popular format.

MAKING THE DUMMY

When working for a publisher it is usual to be given a blank dummy book to work in. This will be in every way as the book will be when published: it will have the same number of pages, be exactly the same size and shape and bound in the same way – the only difference will be that it is blank inside. The illustrator's job is to draw in the dummy how he or she thinks the illustrations will look. This can be done in a rough way, leaving possibilities open to explore in more detailed roughs at a later stage or, more usually, the drawings in the dummy are much as they will be in the printed book, except they are in pencil.

When creating a picture book of your own it is essential to produce a dummy book, because this will enable you to see exactly how your illustrations will look in book form. Therefore one needs to make one. This need not be an elaborate affair; as long as your dummy is the size and scale you want your book to be and it has the correct number of pages, it will be fine. You

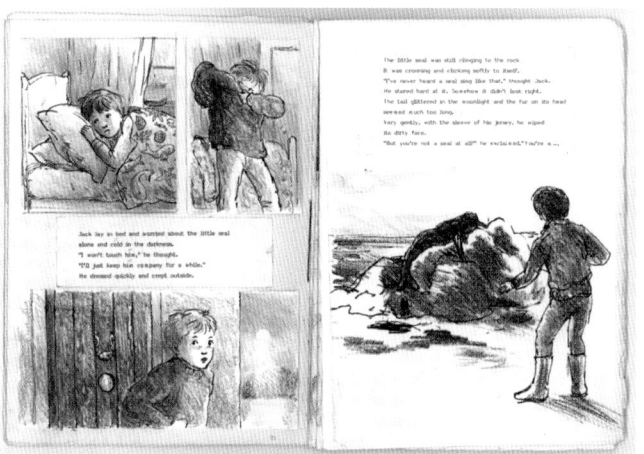

The complete dummy for Carolyn Dinan's picture book *Jack and the Seal Singer*. This is a final dummy and you can see from these beautiful drawings that Carolyn has sorted out everything by this stage. The characters have been created and decided upon, the design of the illustrations on the page has been determined, where the text will go; even the colours have been chosen in this dummy book. The publishers of this book will be in little doubt as to how the artwork will look and any worries or alterations to the story or the pictures that they may require should be raised at this stage.

Looking at the dummy in this way one can see how cleverly Carolyn paces the story. Varying the scale and angles of the illustrations with close-ups, double spreads, and more distant views, Carolyn ensures that the reader is constantly kept engaged and excited by her story. The narrative flow in this series of illustrations never loses momentum – we are carried along to the final image of the story.

can fold two sheets in half three times, as described earlier and either staple the folded sheets together or stitch them onto a simple mull spine (mull is a bookbinder's reinforcing mesh, usually made of calico or fine linen) and then cut them so that the pages open. Alternatively, you might assemble sixteen folded double spreads into a book by sticking them all back to back. The wrap around cover is separate and not counted in the 32 pages so this needs to be added.

How you use the pages is entirely up to you – this is part of the fun of designing your picture book – but you will need a title page that tells us what the book is called and who wrote it. You might want to dedicate the book to someone in which case you need to think about where this will go and, should you intend trying to find a publisher for the book, you will need

stuck swirl 32 cover	tuck swirl is 1 cover	Endpapers 2	3	title 4	page 5	story & starts 6 little	7
8	9	10	11	12	13	14	15
16	17	18	19	20	21	22	23
24	25	26	27	28	29	30	31

This is the pencil dummy for a story I wrote called *Pyewackett*. The story was running long, so the 32 pages that you see here are without endpapers. There is a half title on page 1 followed by a double page title spread on pages 2 and 3, and the book concludes with the credits and copyrights on page 32. This use of the 32 pages is very common.
The story tells of a group of pets that all live in the same close. Gradually throughout the book they begin to disappear. The story concludes with the solving of the mystery of where they have all gone.

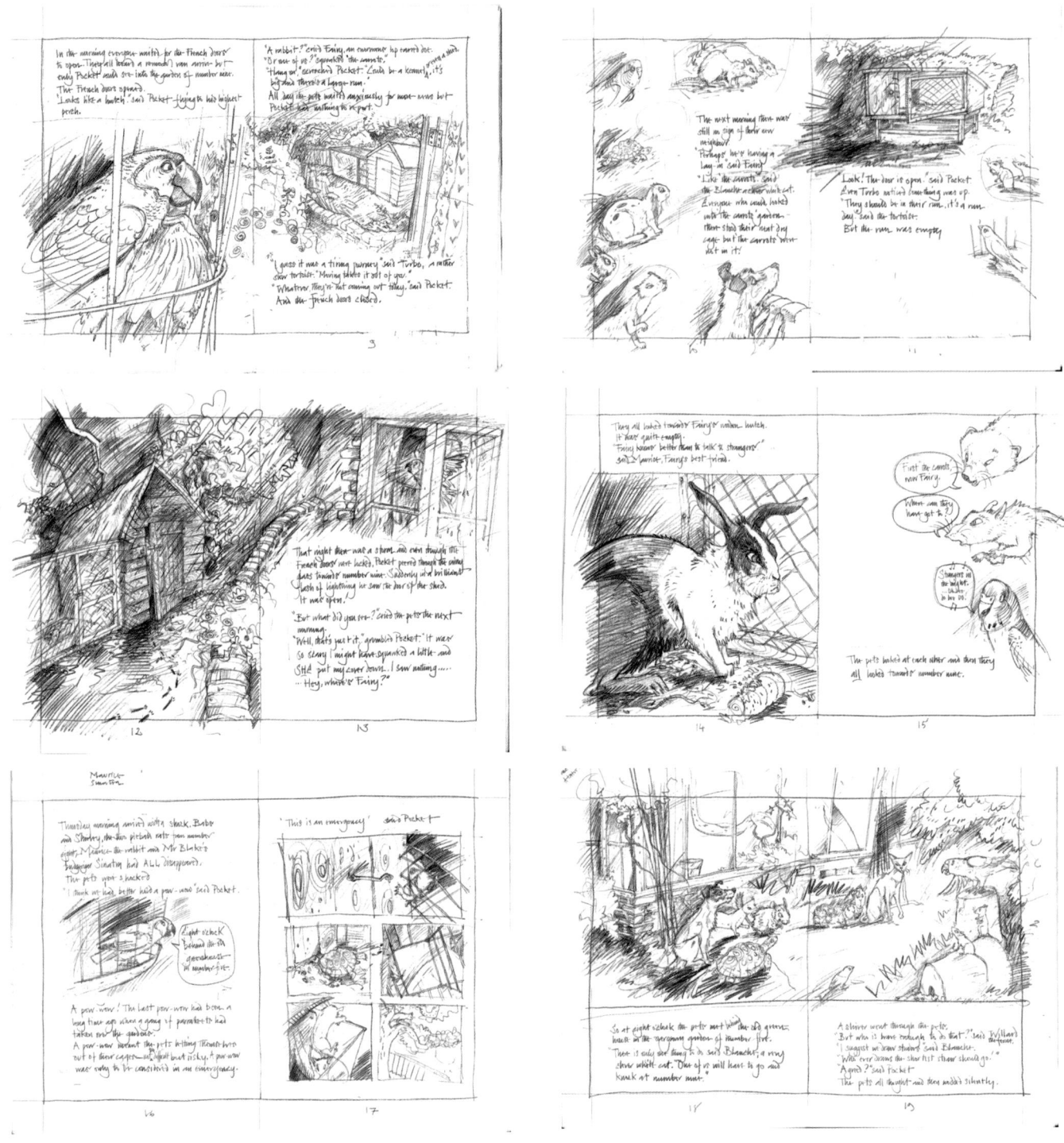

The story begins on page 4 and the first two doubles are used to introduce most of the main characters. By page 8, the third double spread of the story, we are getting to grips with the plot of the book. In any 32-page picture book it is a good idea to do this by the fourth double spread of the story at the latest. By page 12–13 there is the first of the climaxes, with a storm and its following consequences. By pages 18–19, only just over half way through the book, we have another climax and turning point in the story with a secret meeting of the animals. The tension and excitement build over the following spreads until the mystery is solved on pages 26–27.

The remaining two spreads explain and clear up the questions posed by the book.

Working the story out in the dummy in this way is essential. Weaknesses in the narrative or areas of the story that are boring or just do not hold together can be worked on and substituted at this point with the minimum of trouble and reworking. Once the dummy has been approved by the publisher, or is thought to be as perfect as it can be, then one can begin the artwork. There will be a further set of challenges here but the mechanics and ordering of the narrative should not be one of them.

somewhere to put details such as copyright information, and where and when the book is printed and published. You might want the book to have endpapers. (These are double spreads at the beginning and end of your book.) What ever remains is for your story.

Endpapers lend the book a luxurious feel. They can help set the atmosphere for your book and introduce you to what is to follow and likewise wrap up the story at the end. The endpapers are usually double page spreads at the beginning and the end of the book and are usually identical, though they do not have to be. They are often purely decorative but, again, they do not have to be. But the endpapers do need to come out of your 32 pages, so if we look at our 32-page dummy book, pages 2 and 3 and pages 30 and 31 will be the endpapers. Pages 1 and 32, in this case, are stuck to the front and back cover so we will have lost these pages. In a book without endpapers, (like *Pyewackett*), it is not necessary to stick pages 1 and 32 down therefore we have two more pages to play with. It is possible to add the endpapers as extra pages but this will make the book more expensive.

Following the front endpaper is usually the title page and this will often be a double page spread and, in our dummy, pages 4 and 5. Therefore our story will begin on page 6. If we put the copyright details on the left hand side of the title page then we will have twelve double spreads in which to tell our story. If this all sounds complicated and confusing then do not worry: it will soon become apparent how it works when the dummy is in front of you. Secondly, there really are endless combinations of title pages, endpapers, half titles (these are single pages, usually page 1, that are used instead of endpapers and go before the double title page in the absence of endpapers: a half-title begins the *Pyewackett* sequence), so it is very possible to expand or contract the number of available spreads in which to tell the story within the 32-page format. I have shown several possible design layouts but do not be afraid to try out your own; just remember that the front and back cover (the book case) is not included here because it is a separate thing.

DRAWING IN THE DUMMY/ DRAWING OUTSIDE THE DUMMY

The question now is whether to draw directly into your dummy book or to draw on separate paper and then photocopy and stick the drawings in it. There are advantages to both.

By drawing directly in the dummy book one gets a real feeling for how to use the book format to best advantage, in a way that is not always apparent when working on layout paper or in a sketchbook. For example, the right hand pages are dominant:

We see these first when turning the pages of a book but the left hand pages have a surprise value. We can suddenly notice something on the left hand page, especially if it is towards the bottom of the page, that might have escaped our attention on first glance. Some editors will not want text to be at the bottom of a left-hand page for this very reason; apparently children can fail to notice the story here.

The middle of a double page in the dummy book is often referred to as the gutter. Drawing directly in the dummy makes clear the importance of the gutter and its effect on the images that cross the middle. Remember that when books are bound, the stitching or glue used as binding might mean that the pages are pinched in the middle, so a small part of the illustration may disappear. Also, you will remember that when we numbered our folded sheet of paper earlier in this chapter and opened it out again, most of the pages were separated and in flat sheet form did not sit next to their consecutive number. Therefore when the sheet is folded, stitched and cut to make the bound book there is always the possibility (likelihood, even) that images that go across the gutter may not exactly match up. In other words images crossing the gutter may appear to slip up or down. It is difficult to over-stress the importance of the gutter: when designing your illustrations try to avoid any possibility of important information disappearing into the gutter. Images that cross the gutter should do so confidently, and heads and faces must be well into the right or left pages. Limbs that cross the gutter are best if they cross between elbow and wrist or knee and foot – in other words do not have the joint in the gutter as this will look odd.

It is best not to put text across the gutter at all, and always try to avoid words that run over the middle of a spread. Often when working for picture books the publisher will supply you with a grid. The grid will give you a guideline as to where on the page text may be placed and where it may not. Measurements will obviously differ from book to book, but usually there is a minimum of 10cm either side of the gutter where text may not be placed. Likewise one would not want text to appear too near the edges of the page in case they were cropped or lost when the book was printed, trimmed and bound; therefore a further 10cm margin or 'no fly zone' would probably be marked around the entire edge of the double-page spread. By drawing directly into the dummy book all of these pitfalls are made obvious and are therefore easier to rectify.

The disadvantages of working directly in the dummy book are firstly that one may feel cramped and constrained, especially if the book is a small book. Many illustrators like to work proportionally bigger to the actual page size, for example a quarter or half again bigger, even twice bigger. This is explained further in Chapter 7. This is usually marked on the artwork as a quarter up, half up, two up, or s/s, which means the artwork is the same size as it will be in the book. Working proportionally larger means

Here Clare Beaton has drawn out the entire book in a series of small thumbnail sketches on a couple of sheets of layout paper. Small visuals like this may precede a more finished dummy book and one can see that Clare is still playing with different ways of drawing the main characters. Even so, it is evident that Clare is also thinking where the text will go and how the characters will fit into the format of the book. Years of drawing tell here as Clare makes these little visuals look simple and seductive. The visuals are uncomplicated and perfectly clear; we can see what it is that Clare wishes to communicate.

It is extremely difficult to do this succinctly.

that one can fit in more detail. Some media require more space, and some artists simply prefer to work bigger rather than smaller. Providing you have worked out your sizing correctly this is not a problem and the artwork will just be reduced to the correct size, so that it fits in the book, at the proof stage. (If you are drawing directly in the dummy book, this option, at least at this stage, is not available.)

Secondly, if one is working directly in the dummy book there is a limit to how much erasing and re-working the paper will take before it just becomes a dirty mess. Traditionally these initial stages of making a picture book are full of experimentation and exploration of alternative viewpoints, angles, and scenarios. One does not want to feel that one cannot explore every possibility fully before deciding on the best composition. Whilst it is true that if one does destroy the surface of the paper to the point where it is impossible to draw on, one can always stick a fresh piece of paper in, perhaps the very action of drawing in a clean, pristine dummy is inhibiting in itself or at the very least does not encourage experimentation and an open, receptive attitude.

We are all different and different working practices suit different illustrators so try both ways of working. I can think of highly successful illustrators who would never even consider working in anything other than same size, and equally successful illustrators who always work half up, whatever the size of the book.

RESEARCH AND REFERENCE

As has been discussed in previous chapters, having a store of reference is an ongoing activity that never stops. A stack of sketchbooks filled with drawings made directly on location and books and images of relevant reference may need to be consulted. When is the moment for this? Is it before one begins the roughs and dummy book or is it when one begins the artwork? There is no simple answer to this question.

Let us say that our story is about a camel. If one starts off by referring to camels in books before creating the roughs or dummy drawings then it is almost impossible not to be influenced, even dictated to, by the reference that one has found. To

The jacket for *Batty*; here Sarah Dyer plays with the idea of an upside down bat's-eye view of the world. This is quite a daring venture for the cover of a book, but the text and the image of the bat are both large enough to be read whichever way up the book is held.

clarify, if in the reference of a camel the camel is looking towards us, full on, it is likely that one will translate this reference into an illustration where the camel is looking towards us, full on. Of course one does not have to do this; one could – should, even – use the reference more imaginatively. However, there is no point denying what most often happens. This might make the best illustration but it might not, and either way it would have been better to have arrived at the best possible composition independent of the influence of available reference. Nevertheless, drawing a camel from life is difficult enough; drawing a camel from your memory is almost impossible.

A very good way to begin a dummy is to begin it as a vastly scaled down version of your book. If the dummy is small enough initially then the drawings that go in it will be too small to worry about. Details will be irrelevant and one can respond imaginatively with daring compositions and viewpoints without getting bogged down with whether or not the camel's leg looks right. The dummy can be gradually increased in size, feeding in appropriate references along the way where necessary, without losing the initial excitement and dramatic content, until one is working on a full-size dummy.

Reference is very important, particularly drawing on location. One has a much better idea of a place if one has been there and drawn it. However, just because the reference maybe from a specific viewpoint one must always be careful that it does not dictate how the illustration is composed.

In summary, a good beginning for our camel story, before any roughs or dummy work, would be a visit to a zoo. With the knowledge gained from a day drawing camels, watching how they move and react to their environment, one is well equipped to begin a set of drawings for the dummy. Once the initial roughs have been composed it will be more obvious exactly what reference will be needed. This can be gathered and used to realize the roughs.

DESIGNING THE BOOK

The dummy is where everything is created. True, one must first have an idea, then there is the drawing on location and the development of characters and backgrounds, and getting the text right if you are also writing the story. But it is at the dummy book stage that one is forced into deciding exactly what kind of book this is going to be.

The shape of the book

What shape do you want your book to be? There is nothing to stop you having a triangular book or one with five edges (at the time of writing this book I have just seen printed one of my own books in the shape of a circular cake). More usually you will be choosing between a book that is square, landscape or portrait. It may be that your story is about a long journey and that a long landscape format helps emphasize that the characters are travelling a long way through the book. Maybe your story is set in the treetops or is about a giraffe in which case a tall portrait format may be eminently suitable. Perhaps a square format is the one that you like drawing in best. The choice is yours and it will have to be made now.

It is perhaps worth mentioning that some publishers have a less than enthusiastic response to a book that is landscape in format. I have always had a preference for this format but rarely get the chance to push this through, for the reason that landscape books do not easily fit on bookshelves. Whilst waiting to be bought in bookshops they poke out from the shelves and are continually knocked by browsing customers and are therefore gradually shop soiled, the result being that they are then returned to the publisher, unsold, as damaged goods.

The text

It is a fact that very many illustrators do not leave enough room for the story to fit into their books. An illustrator loves drawing pictures, that goes without saying, but a well-designed book should be a marriage between text and image. The one should complement the other. It is useful to leave a little more room for the text than you think you will need. Text that can breathe, and is not cramped, will always look better and therefore so will the illustrations. As an additional point, most published picture books will go into co-editions that are published in other countries. A book that was written in English but then translated and published in German or Dutch may well end up with more words that will need to fit in the area you have left for the text. Whether I have written my own story or am illustrating someone else's story, the first thing I like to do is to go through the text, dividing it into 'chunks' or pieces of text; these might be small paragraphs or even single words. I am thinking where the pictures might be and how I can make the most of my story. How can I make the reader want to turn the page? How can I help the suspense and excitement of my story? If I put this piece of text on page 3 and we turn to page 4 to find what happens does it add to the rhythm of the story? Clearly I cannot have one sentence on page 5 but then so much text on page 6 that there is no room left for a picture at all. These decisions are all part of designing and working out how your picture book will be.

When I have divided up my text I then cut it out and stick it into the dummy with masking tape. I have the option to move it but I am beginning to decide what will go on each page. I am also getting an idea of how much room I will have for the pictures.

PROFILE: LYNN HATZIUS

The Swedish illustrator and designer Lynn Hatzius produces work using found imagery and printed ephemera. Here she talks about working on a collaborative children's book with the German writer Ilke zu Wied.

When I was young my mother, herself a quilt artist and seamstress, provided me with a constant supply of fabrics, papers, and recycled scraps. She encouraged me, and my sisters, to produce all kinds of wonderful handmade bits and pieces. This definitely shaped the way I engaged with the world around me. I constantly collect found material and printed matter to apply to anything from envelopes to personalized books and boxes. I never thought as far as becoming an illustrator but I knew I wanted to follow a creative path. I love the idea of changing something ordinary into something fantastical.

Creating something new, unique and giving life to old scraps of paper excites me immensely. My palette is mostly defined by the collage material I like to use, anything from the subdued browns and greys of old envelopes and newspapers, to snippets of bright colours from magazines and found papers. My collection of ephemeral bits and pieces, old books, catalogues, wrapping papers, in fact any printed matter, grows steadily and forms a vast array of imagery and textures which I can draw on

Lynn Hatzius.

for my illustration work.

I also enjoy using various printmaking techniques, such as etching, wood cut, litho and screen print. Most processes bring with them a certain amount of error or mishap, which excites me immensely. This brings with it the element of surprise and unintended aspect that is brought to a piece of work.

The rough stage of a book is probably the most exciting part. Images seem to form all by themselves from an array of snippets and layers; ideas and meaning crystallize and come together like a puzzle. The next step is a matter of editing, finding an overall style for how the illustrations will work as part of a series or sequence. This part can take a long time and be quite laborious. I think all of the stages in producing a book are vital and enjoyable in their own way. Standing back and looking at the whole book, being ruthless about which details work, and which don't, is essential. Being brave enough to let go of some of the images that might be purely decorative, maybe even distracting and instead committing to those that really capture the essence of the thing and add to the story is also important.

I am currently working on a children's book in collaboration with a German writer. At this point most of the illustrations exist in varying stages of completion. I have been composing them digitally, scanning in material, collaging elements together and rearranging them until they find their place on the page. This way of working gives me the flexibility of going back over the compositions, adding details, simplifying or changing colours and textures. I would say that the computer is a wonderful tool when used in this way but I have found that the illustrations gain far more depth and allure when I re-do them by hand using a mixture of collage and print techniques.

The advantage of a long project like a children's book is that you are able to break from one image and come back to it later. Working on several illustrations at the same time, letting the development of one affect the other, will often produce surprising results. I feel that the same applies to the very nature of freelance work, where deadlines can vary in urgency. In this way sometimes a number of projects can coincide and the work from one can inform another. This challenges a constant flow of new approaches and ways of creating fresh imagery.

Alternating between my desk at home, the studio I share with my sister and the print workshop provides me with surroundings that feel different and affect my work in different, unique ways. In this way a change in the workplace can help me get a new boost of inspiration too. Regular breaks, walks, travelling, a visit to a bookshop, an exhibition, a market, a charity shop, watching a film – in fact any sort of stimulation – can trigger a creative thought and sow a seed that will grow, often subconsciously, until it blossoms into a distinct idea waiting to be put onto paper.

Regarding illustrators I like, I am very fond of the German illustrator Wolf Erlbruch and like his simple but striking compositions, wonderful humour and his beautiful mix of drawing and collage. I have always been taken by the boldness of the Czech artist Kveta Pacovská's brightly coloured characters and compositions and the way they find their place into wonderful book formats. I love the Swedish illustrator Elsa Beskow's magical scenes of trolls, fairies and forest life and likewise Sibille von Olfers' work. They make me feel like a little girl lost in a miniature world hidden at the bottom of a garden.

It is not a good idea to have text running over an image. Try to keep all of the text well away from any of the illustration. Very often an illustrator will want to run a pale wash, extending it from the main illustration, so that it runs behind the text and therefore avoiding a harsh edge to the illustration. This is especially the case where the book is comprised of large double-page illustrations. Picture books are usually for children and children who are learning to read; this is hard enough without having text that is difficult to see. There is a strong argument for always having the text on the white of the page and never having a tint running behind it.

Text that you want to have in a lighter colour than the background (for example, white text over a black background) is a separate issue which will be discussed later.

The pictures

At some point a decision will have to be made as to how the pictures will fit into the book. Will they run off over the edge of the page? Will they be in frames or boxes, contained and surrounded by the page itself? Will they be vignettes that have a faded edge that evaporates into nothing before our eyes? Will they all be double spreads or singles with text on one side? Will they be a mixture of all of these things?

Of course you could begin just drawing the illustrations and then experiment with some of these design permutations with photocopies after they are done. It is a great idea to have a window mount with the window cut to page size and move this over the rough drawing, thereby exploring and discovering potentially exciting compositions. (Here is another reason for not drawing directly in the dummy.) However, I think it helps to try and imagine what kind of book you want to make, because how one contains the illustrations on the page will make an enormous difference to the style and appearance of the book. A series of large double spreads looks luxurious and puts the emphasis firmly on the pictures. It allows the illustrator to really go to town and wallow in the atmosphere of the book. It also creates a measured pace. If all of the illustrations are double-page spreads it is more difficult to play with time and speed in the way that a series of small vignettes all on one page might do, adding an animated quality to part of the book.

A book with lots of little vignettes or frames (boxed images) will give the book a feeling of time passing. It takes discipline and commitment to keep an even standard throughout an entire picture book when working like this. Also, it can make the book feel long, like going on a journey, and one does not want the reader to get bored or wish one would just 'get on'. Great skill is needed to keep the reader interested and avid. Changing the scale of the frames or vignettes will introduce variety and

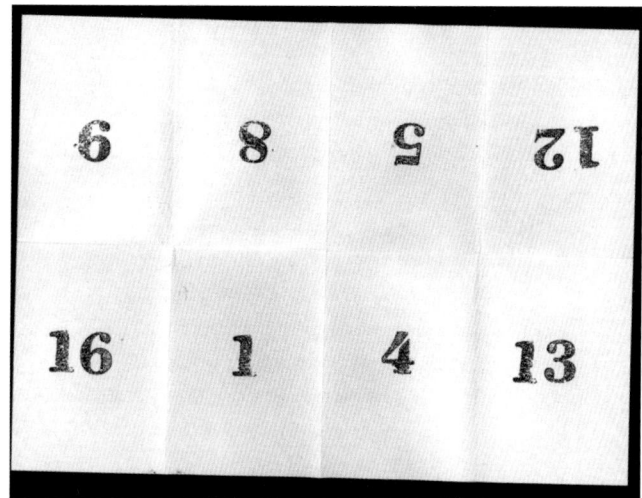
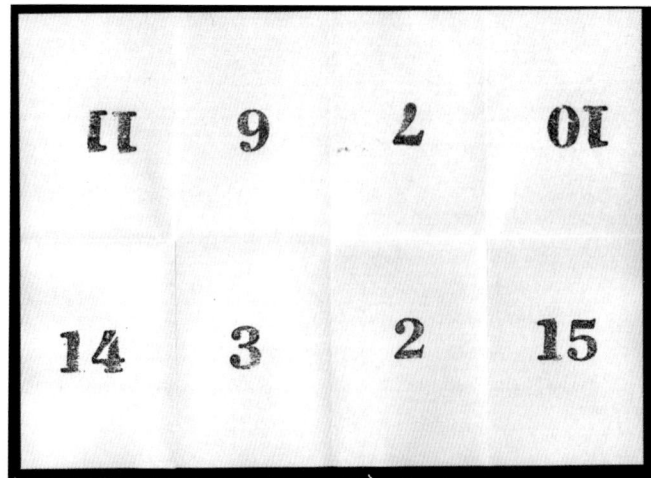

Numbered sheets showing the order of pages. When folded in half three times, stapled or sewn and cut, this A3 sheet will make a small 16-page book.

surprise. Popping in the odd full-page frame or double spread can be very effective in infusing the book with energy and curtailing any feeling of monotony.

Having the text on one side of a double-page spread and the picture on the opposing page was once the standard way of producing a children's picture book and it was because the colour illustrations needed to be printed on different, more expensive paper. This is not the case now, and books designed to this format can look old fashioned and static. It could prove difficult to change the rhythm of your story, as fast, exciting parts of the story will be getting exactly the same treatment as descriptive calmer passages. Looking at it another way, these kinds of pictures have a classic, smart feel. This format is a great vehicle for highly detailed work, perhaps the kind of book where one is looking for something in the pictures, counting, or trying to spot a character.

PROJECT FOURTEEN: HALF-SIZE DUMMY

Take a piece of A3 paper, fold it in half three times and staple it in the middle. This form of binding is called saddle stitch. Cut the pages that are folded so that you have a book A6 in size and with sixteen pages (the covers back and front are included in this).

Now find a short story, memory or incident that you want to illustrate and adapt it to fit into your book. Draw directly in the dummy book. You might need to edit the text, which can be handwritten in the book or typed and stuck in. Think up a title. On page one create a cover, although if you are really short of space you may also begin the story here.

When you are drawing in the book try to make it so that the reader really wants to turn the page. Think of the format and how you use the various ways of containing the illustrations on the page. Keep it simple, and it is probably best to keep it black and white.

The sixteen pages that are in this little dummy make it half the length of most children's picture books. Nevertheless, sustaining the quality of the roughs from beginning to end, with no falling off of standard, will be a challenge.

PROJECT FIFTEEN: LONG, TALL, SHORT, SQUARE

Using a variety of different sizes of paper, fold each in half three times, stapling or stitching the books so that you end up with a selection of differently shaped books: landscape, tall portrait, square, and so on.

Taking a simple story that will fit into your sixteen pages, try it out by drawing it in the different formats. Analyse what you do and do not like about each. Is it that one particular format suits your story more than the others, and if so, why? Is it that you just prefer one of the formats for drawing in, regardless of the requirements of the story?

This is a good exercise for finding out what suits your drawings and how to get the best out of them.

PROJECT SIXTEEN: A PRINTED STORY

Take a sheet of A3 paper and fold it in half three times. Number the pages one to sixteen. Now open the sheet out.

Measuring the pages as double spreads, draw out eight frames to these measurements on another sheet of good quality paper, each frame surrounded by white paper. Number these frames with a small pencil in the top left and right hand corner of each page. All eight frames are as double spreads so page 16 will be the left-hand half of page 1, then 2 and 3, 4 and 5 and so on.

Now choose a story to illustrate throughout these pages. You might want to use colour.

When you have illustrated the entire book cut up the illustrations as necessary and assemble them onto your original sheet of paper so that they now sit in the order it dictates. You will find that page 4 sits between page 1 and 13 and has page 3 on the back of it. It might help to look at the accompanying illustrations.

If your measurement of the page size was accurate they will all fit on the two sides of your original A3 sheet of paper. If your measuring was not accurate then you might have to trim or make up the edges.

Now take this sheet along to a photocopier and photocopy it onto double-sided A3 paper. You should end up with a printed copy of your A3 artwork sheet. Carefully fold the photocopied sheet three times, staple it or stitch it, cut and trim the pages. You will have a small A6 16-page illustrated book. It should be easy to see the effect of the gutter when making a book this way. A book that is professionally published and printed will not show the effect of this quite as dramatically, but the principle is basically the same.

P.16-17
What should she be wearing - night clothes or her outdoor things?

This pencil rough is from *Nightmare* by Berlie Doherty. When working on the roughs for this ghost story I thought it was important to try and capture something of the excitement and fear that resonates through the book. Set on a frozen, bleak, northern moor this thrilling part of the story shows the main character galloping through the sky on a phantom stallion with her companion and friend, himself a ghost!

A wonderful assortment of media but of course the real beauty of these tools is in what they might be made to create.

Chapter Six
MEDIA and
MATERIALS

Inevitably, when making an illustration, you are going to have to decide what to make your illustration with and what to make it on. It would be easy to fill every page in this book talking about media and materials and how to use them but this makes too much of it because what is important is the illustration itself. How one arrives at it successfully does not matter; it only matters that one does arrive at it. It is as well therefore to say here that if an illustration is not going as well as one would hope it is probably not the fault of the materials you are using. When using media it is vital to experiment and explore ways of getting it to do what you want. You may find a way of working with it that is different from everyone else and perhaps it will be this that gives your work a particular ambience, or quality.

That said, it might be useful to know a little of what is available and some of the ways of getting the best out of it but again, it is up to you to test the possibilities of your media. Like all tools they will only respond to your instruction. Do not be afraid to go against the norm, as there really is never just one way of using anything.

USING QUALITY MATERIALS / SCANNING ONTO THE COMPUTER

Many illustrators work by drawing freely in their sketchbook, often without any clear idea of what they are aiming for and then scan this image onto a computer to develop and work on further, thus creating the final image. This is fine and not only does it take the pressure out of producing a piece of artwork but it can lead to spontaneous and lively illustration; it is a way of working that suits many illustrators. However, it is also worth adding that investing in quality materials and using these brings with it its own advantage.

There is no point in denying that artists' materials can be quite expensive. Paints usually last a very long time and as most illustrators work for commissioned books and magazines, where the size of illustration rarely exceeds A3, paper also is relatively long lasting, especially when bought by the ream (480 sheets). It is usually cheaper to buy materials in larger quantities if you can and buying paper by the ream or pack will work out considerably cheaper than buying it by the sheet.

There is a tension to working on a fine piece of quality watercolour paper with good quality materials that can lift an illustration into something special. One does not want this to become intimidating but, rather as an actor might rise to the occasion of a packed house or a sportsman to a big race, there is something to working with quality materials that is hard to replicate. One wants the illustration to succeed because one has gone to the trouble and expense of buying quality materials; furthermore they are a delight to use. One does not want the illustration to turn out badly and negate all of this effort; therefore one concentrates hard and gives the thing one's full attention and hopefully the end result of all of this is a stunning illustration. This issue is discussed further in Chapter 7, but it is worth stating again here, try not to underestimate the effect that using decent materials can have on your work.

PAPER

There are endless varieties of paper to choose from and each illustrator will find a paper that suits them. A few basic guidelines are given here.

Quality drawing paper is usually classified in three ways:

- Rough, or grain torchon in French;
- CP/Cold pressed, or grain fin in French;
- HP/Hot pressed, or grain satine in French.

Sometimes there is the addition of the word 'not', which refers to the surface of the paper not being rough (bizarre but true). These paper classifications more or less speak for themselves. Hot pressed paper is a very smooth paper with no discernible surface to it at all. Cold pressed paper has a slight surface but is still good for pen and wash, CP (not) being even more suitable. Rough paper has a textured surface suitable for heavy watercolour washes.

Paper usually has one 'good' side and this can be determined by looking for the watermark. If this can be read then this is the 'good' side; if the writing is backwards then this is the back of the paper. Of course you may prefer to use the back of the paper, which is fine.

Think what you want to use on the paper before you buy it. If you are using watercolour you will need a paper that is white – the whiter the better if you want the colours to be fresh and vibrant. If you wish to use a dip pen and ink then the paper will need to be smooth. Smooth paper tends not to be so absorbent so if you are planning to draw in ink with a brush then the ink will be slow to dry. Smooth paper is more suited to mapping pens that scratch the paper, allowing the ink to penetrate.

If you want to use watercolour over a pencil drawing then a rougher surface will suit. If you want to use a lot of water on your paper then it will need to be of a substantial weight, 410gsm (200lb) or heavier, so that the paper does not wrinkle and buckle when wet causing the paint to 'pool' in the valleys. Bristol board is a flexible board made from layers of paper so it is good for watercolour, if not used too wet, and yet smooth enough for pen work. It has a rougher side that may be pre-

Papageno by Lynn Hatzius. In this vibrant illustration Lynn uses the medium of collage to brilliant effect, catching the excitement and exuberance of this comic character from Mozart's *The Magic Flute*. Lynn's stunning use of colour and her star-studded sky, which echoes the 1816 Karl Schinkel set designs for the Palace of the Queen of the Night, both help make this a magical and thrilling piece of illustration.

ferred and is flexible enough to wrap around a scanning drum if needed.

Layout paper is excellent for rough work. The paper is thin and relatively see-through, especially when used on a light box. Good quality layout paper will take ink, markers and pencil and even a light wash.

Ingres paper and sugar paper are not suitable for watercolour but may be suitable for pastels and gouache where the colour of the paper will not adversely affect the quality and colour of the paint. Ingres paper is particularly useful for illustrations where the subject is white as one can see what one is painting. Manila board, originally made from hemp and yellow in colour is usually the paper used for making stencils. It is strong and coated with a solution of turpentine and linseed oil to make it waterproof. The combination of these two substances on the

board needs careful handling and the prepared board should not be stored as there is the possibility of spontaneous combustion.

WATERCOLOUR

Watercolour is probably one of the most versatile media but also one of the most difficult to use effectively as it does not allow for much alteration or correction and is easily overworked. You can get by with a palette of twelve colours and the colours you choose will obviously help define the look and atmosphere of your work. For example, when one thinks of the illustrations of Arthur Rackham one immediately thinks of the sepia and umber washes that he uses again and again, whereas Michael Foreman's illustrations usually draw on a much more intense and vibrant set of colours.

Watercolours can be expensive but they do last a long time and you do not need that many. As a general rule you get what you pay for, and it is worth buying good quality colours that are clear and translucent and not milky.

It is a good idea to limit the number of different colours you use in one illustration, as a limited palette is usually more effective. Imagine a red poppy in a field of green and the same red poppy in a multi-coloured bouquet. The value of the colour is more appreciated when used effectively.

Usually when using watercolour one does not use white or black. Black is much more effective when it is mixed from the colours in your palette (Payne's Grey and Sepia make a rich, warm black), and white is the paper. White watercolour cannot be completely clear or translucent and will make your colours cloudy and dull. Watercolour relies on the whiteness of the paper to give the colours their luminosity and brilliance; there-

Watercolours.

fore anything, like white, that cuts down the light coming from the paper, is best avoided. Therefore when putting your palette together it is worth remembering that with watercolour you cannot mix a pink; just by adding more water to red you will not get pink, just a more faded watery red. You will have to buy a pink if you want it as one of the colours in your palette. The same goes for light blue or lemon yellow. Remember also that if you are after bright, clear, intense colour the whiter the paper the more likely it is that you will achieve this. A cream or an off-white paper will certainly dull down your colours, but then of course this might be what you are after.

When you buy watercolours you can often purchase them in a box containing a selected palette that has been chosen for you. It is not a bad idea to start with this. A good manufacturer will have put together a basic palette containing a suitable mix of colours that will enable you to produce a further extensive range of colours by mixing them together. For some reason manufacturers usually include a black and a Chinese white in this selection. I would replace these. As your experience grows you will inevitably replace or add colours that are more to your liking.

This is not a book about watercolour or even materials and media, as there are plenty of books available on these subjects should you feel the need for them. Nevertheless, as I am often asked to recommend a small but complete palette I have listed below a palette of twelve colours, which will enable you to mix a myriad of further hues for the minimum outlay. I have given specific named colours but clearly these can be substituted for preferred shades of the same colour (for example, you might prefer Vandyke Brown to Burnt Umber or Sepia) but in a limited palette you probably will not want three browns.

Cerulean Blue
Rose Madder
Burnt Umber
Yellow Ochre
Payne's Grey
French Ultramarine
Lemon Yellow
New Gamboge
Viridian Green
Cadmium Red
Crimson Alizarin
Naples Yellow

The use of ox gall, which one can buy from most art shops, may help keep the watercolour workable for longer. Ox gall is a wetting agent and a few drops are usually added to the mixed colour. It smells horrible.

OIL PAINT

There is no real reason why one should not use oil colour for illustration work, yet somehow not many illustrators do use it. It takes a long while to dry: putting oil paintings in the freezer helps this process; heat will delay it. If working on board, not canvas, be aware that many scanning processes require the artwork to be scanned around a circular drum, therefore the illustration needs to be flexible.

Oil paint allows the possibility of working over and over the image, unlike watercolour. Therefore an image can gradually emerge and be altered almost indefinitely. Again, as with watercolour, there are entire books dealing with ways of using oil colour that can be readily consulted. Suffice to say, this is an exciting and under-used medium in children's illustration.

PENCILS

Pencils, whether coloured or graphite, are probably the media we became most familiar with as children and therefore often the media we can feel confident and comfortable with, especially if we are just beginning to think of illustrating a children's book.

The softness of pencils is often the thing that many illustrators look for. Pencils are graded 6H (very hard) to 6B (very soft), with HB sitting in the middle. The soft pencils will give you a greater tonal range; the hard pencils a faint grey but precise line. Soft pencils kept sharp can give a fine line providing you do not press too hard.

Colouring pencils bring with them memories of childhood and I think this is why so many of us are not daunted by them,

Colouring pencils.

feeling instead that they will not require years of practice to get good at, like maybe watercolour or oils. However, they are difficult to blend and slow to use and can look constrained. Personally I think they work best as one element in a mixed media illustration.

PENS

Dip pens and mapping pens are amongst the most popular drawing tools and many children's illustrators use them. There is a large selection of different nibs, from flexible nibs (like the Gillott 303 and 192) which can give an expressive, exciting and

These old boxes of mapping pens are decorative and desirable objects. There is an endless variety of different nib sizes from fine points to broad, italic to ball point. Part of the fun of using these nibs is experimenting with them and finding out what kind of line you can get out of them.

These vintage nibs were made sometimes going through as many as sixteen different processes. In today's ruthless and cost-efficient market, nibs are mass-produced by machine and do not compare in any way to these vintage wonders. In any case, fine liners have to a large extent become an easier, yet less expressive, substitute.

varied line) to crow quills (like the Gillott 659), which offer more stability. Dip pens take practice and experience but the rewards are great and their unpredictability lends a liveliness to a line which is difficult to get with any other tool.

When using a dip pen one needs the ink to be fluid and this often means 'watering' it. A bottle of drawing ink left open on a desk day in, day out will become thick and sticky, making it impossible to get versatility out of the nib. Pour a quarter of the ink into another bottle for later use, and top up the remaining ink with distilled or boiled water. The ink will remain waterproof and travel much more readily over the paper. As the ink is used this process can be repeated, as an open bottle of ink will gradually thicken again over time. When black Indian ink is looking grey, or more usually brown, it is time to invest in a new bottle of ink but this does take a long time.

The nib needs to go into the ink enough to cover just the top half of the nib; there is no advantage pushing the nib in up to the handle. Wiping the nib with a tissue before it is re-dipped each time might seem annoying but it does keep the nib free of old dry ink and therefore able to make fine and thick lines easily. It will eventually become a habit that one does not even notice and it is good practice.

When using dip pens the paper needs to be smooth enough to allow the pen to travel over it without sticking or skipping, therefore heavy rough watercolour papers are not suitable for dip pens.

Fountain pens are fabulous to draw with as they do not have the unpredictability of dip pens or the added complications of the bottle of ink and of keeping the nib clean and replenished with ink. However, they will not give such an expressive line and remember that if you wish to add colour washes you will need to use waterproof ink such as Fount India.

Fineliners and rotring pens will give you a line of one thickness, so they are better suited to drawing of a more technical nature or diagrams. However, they are far easier to control than dip pens and therefore more popular with beginners. Lines can be thickened either by going over and over them or by using a range of different point sizes. If you are thinking of adding colour make sure that the ink in the pens is waterproof.

ACRYLICS AND GOUACHE

Acrylics allow for working over and adjusting. They do not 'pick up' so, rather like oil paint, an illustration can evolve on the page, changing and refining as it goes. This would be impossible with watercolour. As the paint is not translucent the colour and tint of the paper will not adversely affect the colours on the page.

Gouache is usually mixed to a consistency resembling single

Reels of cotton in Clare Beaton's Studio.

cream and put down evenly. It does 'pick up' when worked over so one needs to use it with confidence and purpose. This is a medium that has rather gone out of fashion in recent years but its milky opaque quality can look stunning when used well. The paint has an inner light of its own and a very distinctive quality that is instantly recognizable.

COLLAGE

Collage is the act of building up an image using pieces of cut paper or cloth. It is a medium that has seen a real revival in recent years and is now very popular among new illustrators.

The feel of your illustration will depend in part on what collage material you use. You may want to collect papers and fabrics. You may indeed have a fondness for a particular style of material or era in which the patterns were used. Of course you can create your own collage material by painting various papers in a variety of shades, stippling, putting the colour down roughly or smoothly, tearing up magazines, even introducing photomontage.

As with all of these things it is easier to work from a healthy store of materials rather than wait until one needs a particular paper and try to find it, so storing and collecting collage material needs to be something that you do continually if you want to work in this medium.

You will probably find it useful to keep to a limited palette (this could equally apply to whatever media you are using but particularly with collage). It is easy to lose the image in a riot of coloured papers and patterns. In fact one of the main skills when working with collage is to produce an image that is clear and easily read.

Roughs in collage

A difficulty when using collage is exactly how one produces a rough, indeed how one explores the illustration, composition, viewpoint, angles, without actually producing the artwork. A pencil rough can be used to explore the content of an idea but clearly if collage or photomontage is to be the chosen medium then one is at the mercy of what collage material one has got available. Any rough produced may differ so widely from the eventual artwork as to be almost worthless.

Having known several successful illustrators who work in this medium I can say that each approaches this dilemma differently. As can be read in Clare Beaton's profile in Chapter 7, she does in fact produce a careful and accurate rough and the artwork mirrors the rough. Other illustrators, especially those who use photomontage, may decide to produce the artwork but photocopy this in black and white, at the rough stage. Of course, should alterations need to be made – which is highly likely, almost inevitable – they will then need to produce another piece of artwork entirely.

Here Emma Block uses collage very effectively to capture the lightness and prettiness of an English tea for her book *Tea and Cakes*.

MIXED MEDIA

Instead of using one particular medium many illustrators prefer to use everything and anything when creating an image. Using mixed media can provide exciting and vibrant illustration, breaking all the rules and accepted practice in trying to realize an imagined effect.

Making an illustration using mixed media and then perhaps scanning the image onto the computer to develop it further can be a rewarding and refreshing way of working.

PRINT

You may be interested in using print as a way of making your illustrations. It would be easy to talk for the entire length of this book on print-making techniques. Indeed there are many books that deal with this subject. A few options are outlined here.

Lino cut, wood cut and the finer wood engraving can all be achieved at home and involve drawing, with the appropriate tools, into either lino or wood, thereby leaving proud the image one wishes to print. This is inked up with a roller and, in the absence of a press, a reasonable image can be successfully made by rubbing over the paper with the back of a spoon, once it is on the 'image block'.

Etching and dry point, where the image is carved out of the plate, and the ink rubbed in the cuts, will need a roller press to print a reasonable image. Therefore these are not so easily produced at home – unless one has a press of course.

Monoprints are easy to make at home. Roll the ink over a sheet of Perspex; water-based ink is fine but oil-based ink is better as you have longer to play at making the image before the ink dries, making a thin coat. Newspaper placed around the edges of the plate will give you a clean, sharp edge. Drop the paper gently onto the Perspex. Draw the image line through the back of the paper. When you lift your paper off, the image will appear in ink on the reverse side. It is called a monoprint because you get only one print.

There are various techniques of producing an illustration through monoprint. Drawing directly into the ink with scrunched up newspaper or a sharp pointed instrument can lay a foundation for an image or produce an image in its own right. Wire wool and a palette knife, which can be scraped into the ink, are also useful tools to draw with. Coloured inks can be used and masks can be applied to the Perspex so that areas of ink do not mark the paper.

PROJECT SEVENTEEN: GETTING TO KNOW YOUR PALETTE

A very good way of getting to know what you can get from your colours is to explore every possible combination. This record can be kept for reference.

Preferably in a sketchbook draw yourself a grid of boxes representing the number of colours in your palette. Therefore a box of twelve colours will have twelve boxes all 4cm × 4cm drawn across one double spread. Repeat this for the number of colours in your palette, so there will be twelve double page spreads each with twelve boxes 4cm × 4cm.

Now choose a colour from your palette, let us say Cerulean Blue, and fill in the first box. This page will be titled Cerulean Blue. In the second box mix it with one of the other colours in your palette, keeping the blue to one corner and the other colour to the opposite corner but mixing the two colours in the box. The idea is to get the variety of different colour shades available by mixing these two colours. Call this box Cerulean Blue and whatever you have used. Fill the remaining squares with the other colours each mixed with Cerulean Blue.

On the second page choose another colour from your palette and repeat this process by mixing it in turn with all of the other colours. The completed book will show you every combination of every two colours in your palette.

It is possible to extend this to three colours using larger boxes but even mixing two colours, as here, will surprise you with unlikely results.

PROJECT EIGHTEEN: SAME THING, DIFFERENT MEDIA

A way of getting to know a variety of different media and the kind of effect they will produce is to draw the same thing but using different media each time.

Work from a rough or small visual that you are happy with and avoid anything too involved or complex. Draw the image on different papers using different media, maybe jotting down things you notice about how the media responds; for example, is the paper too absorbent for a fine liner, or does the ink of a dip pen bleed?

Getting the best out of your materials and getting the effect you want comes with experience. It is only by using materials that one finds out what they will do. Looking at how illustrators work and finding out what they use will also help you. To look properly at how illustrators work one does need to see the original artwork; a printed version does not always give up these secrets. Illustrators' work is often available to see in galleries and more specialist museums.

Monoprints by Carolyn Dinan.

PROFILE: EMMA BLOCK

Emma Block.

Emma Block makes her illustrations using a variety of different media and here she describes the processes she goes through.

I always start with sketchbooks, lots of sketchbooks, and I prefer thin stitched sketchbooks because they are easy to scan, not hardback books, which can be awkward. When creating a piece of artwork I either trace or scan, in pencil at this point, from the original image in the sketchbook, so this original image stays very much part of the artwork. This means that in my sketchbooks I only ever draw on one side of the paper. I try to draw from life as much as possible as it will bring a quality to my work that is difficult to get any other way. If I do not have what I need in my sketchbooks and cannot, for whatever reason, go on location to draw, then I may draw from photographic reference. When I was working on some illustrations for *The Secret Garden* I went to Melford Hall (Beatrix Potter used to draw there). Next I think about the colours I will use. I have a large stash of different papers, all colours and patterns, and I try these out by putting them behind a tracing of the image. Looking through my paper stacks I try to visualize which colours will go together. I have a particular fondness for brown paper, folders and envelopes. Greys are another favourite and then aquamarine and turquoise. I love this part of the process and enjoy especially the 'hands on' nature of it, although some people might do this part of it in Photoshop.

Having started with the drawing, and cut out all the individual pieces of paper that I am going to use, I sometimes also paint the paper with acrylics. As a foundation for all of this I often use a paper called Rhino Poo paper. I buy this in large sheets. I put all of the shadows in with ink, details can also be added in this way with ink or acrylic. It all has to be stuck together and I sometimes scan in a background digitally. I find scanning in the background really helps as I originally struggled with this part of the process and scanning in individual pieces of paper which can be cut out and arranged in photoshop allows for experimentation and the opportunity to change my mind many times over.

When choosing whether to work at an enlarged size or not I try to choose a size that feels natural. Working in the way I do means I do not like to work too small. I can tell if the illustration is going to be successful or not sometimes by a little feeling that it is right but sometimes by putting the illustration away and looking at it again a few days after; then I instantly know if it works or not. Another useful way of seeing the illustration afresh is to hold it up to a mirror.

Working on the artwork is my favourite part of illustrating. By the time I get to work on the artwork I more or less know what I am doing; most of the problems are solved and sorted by this stage. I love telling a story with my illustrations and children's books allow me to do just this. I would like my readers to feel that my illustrations fit with the text but also that they carry my own ideas. It is important that the illustrations are more than just decorative and that they also reflect some of the thoughts I have had on reading the book.

Most of my work draws inspiration from the past and I like capturing a sense of place. I find inspiration in old films and vintage clothes so this kind of subject matter forms a large part of my sketchbooks. I think books are very important in childhood and a really good children's book has a great longevity.

In these six double page spreads from a sketchbook of mine I am exploring, with a variety of different media, the old monarch mnemonic WILLY, WILLY, HARRY, STE. Anything goes in here. There are hand cut rubber stamps, gouache, watercolour, inks, collage, pva, printed ephemera and acrylic. The final illustrations that evolved from this KINGS sketchbook I used to promote my new website and they formed the beginning of an on going project to create various forms of illustration and ephemera representing every monarch that has sat on the English throne. That works out at 76 monarchs.

Here is a finished illustration from *Who Really Killed Cock Robin?*, a story for older children based around the very old nursery rhyme, 'Who Killed Cock Robin?' This double-page spread is for the verse, 'Who'll fetch the link? "I," said the Linnet, "I'll fetch it in a minute".' Many of the roughs for this book are included in Chapter 9. The illustration is pen and watercolour.

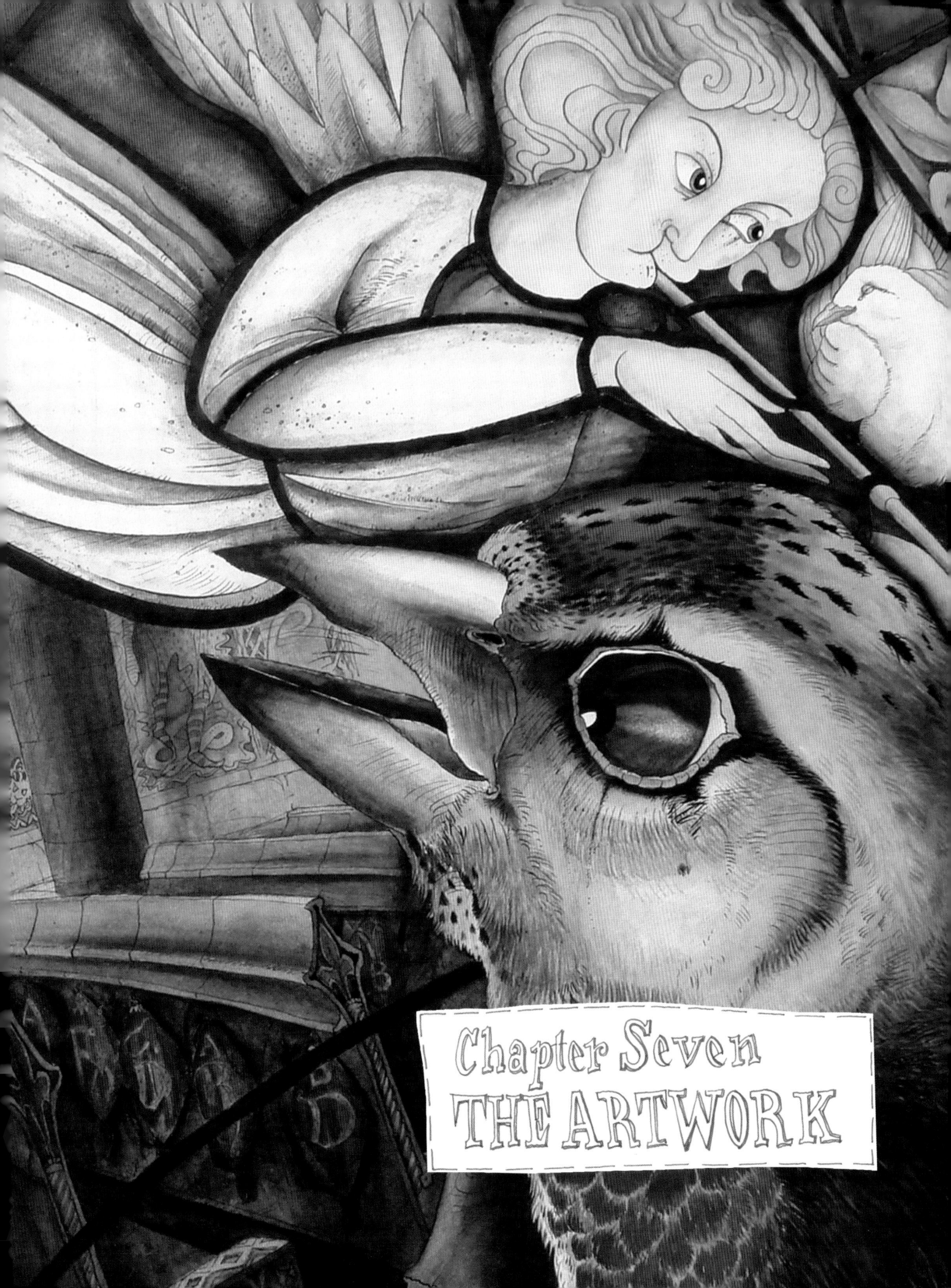

Chapter Seven
THE ARTWORK

Working on the finished illustrations for your story is probably the part of the whole process that has been most eagerly looked forward to. Painting the pictures, deciding on the colours, working with your chosen media, these are the things that one probably thought of doing at the very beginning of the whole project of illustrating a children's picture book. However, as will by now be obvious, this is just one stage in the process of illustrating a book and already an entire series of decisions will have been made and problems solved, so that by the time one is ready to begin the artwork, one would hope to have a pretty good idea of exactly what kind of a book this is going to be.

SIZE

As was discussed previously, you may prefer to work on the artwork at a larger scale than that which will appear in the book. This might enable you to include more detail, or it might be that the media you are using suits a larger scale, or perhaps you just like working on larger paper.

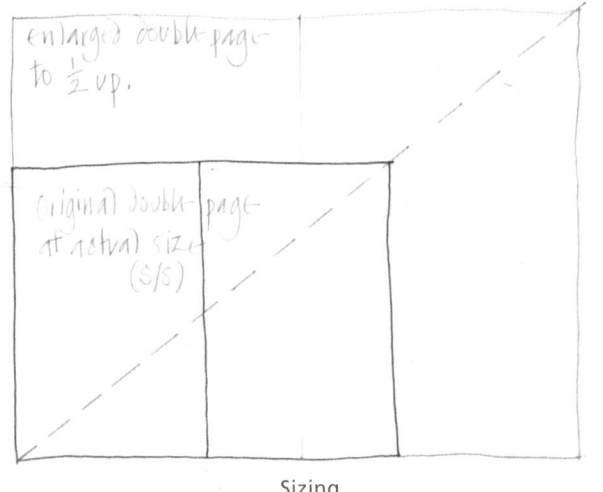

Sizing.

Obviously the proportion of the pages must remain the same, as this enlarged artwork is going to have to be reduced at the scanning and printing stage. We will not be able to fit an illustration that has changed shape into our desired size of book. The most commonly worked up sizes are one quarter up, one half up and two up and the calculation is simple and the same for all.

To work half up, measure the size of your double spread. Now divide the length measurement in half and add half again to the length. Measure the width of the double spread and add half the width measurement again to the width. This will give you the size of your double spread at half up. To check if you have worked this enlargement out correctly, an imaginary line drawn from the bottom left hand corner of your double spread travelling diagonally across the page passing through the top right hand corner of the right hand page should also extend to cross directly through the top right hand corner of the enlarged page size. To work out an enlargement on a quarter up or two up the added measurement is a quarter of the double page length and width, or double the measurement length and width respectively.

A word of warning: when working bigger than the original page size be aware that your illustration will look different when reduced. Experience will soon enable you to judge exactly how the illustration might change when reduced down, so until you gain this experience it may help to photocopy your artwork as you go. The characteristics of your chosen page size are exaggerated when one enlarges them. A landscape book will look very much longer and thinner when worked two up, as a tall portrait shape will look taller.

A further point worth mentioning here is that if your enlargement takes your page size beyond A3 it is possible your artwork may have to be cut in half in order to scan the illustration. Even A3 scanners are rare things. You do have the option to have your illustrations photographed but this can be an expensive solution and the quality of the image printed may be affected. This happens especially easily with landscape books: a long book enlarged soon exceeds the dimensions of A3.

Endpaper from *The Girl with the Bird's Nest Hair* by Sarah Dyer.

THE BLEED

The 'bleed' is the area by which the illustration exceeds the page size and is important because if one only works to the exact area of the page size then, when the illustration is printed, there is a very real possibility – even likelihood – that a small area of white will appear around the page edge, making for an untidy book.

It is good practice, and a contractual obligation, when producing artwork to always have a 5mm or 10mm bleed around the entire double spread. Your illustration should extend to this bleed so that when it is printed the colour runs right to the edge of the page throughout. Avoid any important details near the page edge.

If you are using vignettes or frames to box your illustrations then make sure you keep the vignettes or frames well within the page size. Do not work too close to the page edge but allow at least 5mm between your illustration and the page edge, a kind of reverse bleed.

PAPER SIZE

When producing artwork always work on paper that is larger than the size of the double spread. There are several reasons for this. Most obviously, when the illustration is handled it may become grubby and marked therefore it seems obvious to have an area around the illustration where it maybe picked up and handled without worry of the artwork being affected. The artwork maybe knocked or dropped in which case a dented or damaged corner will not matter.

Throughout this book we have looked at the different stages involved in the creation of Wesley Robin's award winning *Train* book. We have seen some of the early ideas sheets, some of the sketchbook drawings and some of the roughs. Here is some of Wesley's artwork that has been copied, cut out and assembled. The original idea for this book was to have it in the shape of a train with the pages as the carriages. Our journey through the book is a journey through the train itself.

It is essential to write on the artwork your name, address, contact details, what the illustration is for, the page number and the enlargement size, for example half-up, or S/S if you have worked same size. You should also mark up the artwork with registration marks – these appear outside the page area. Registration marks are small horizontal and vertical ink lines, to tell the printer the exact size of the page and where to crop it, therefore they need to be accurate. Usually the publisher will 'mark up' the artwork for you, following your pencil guide. If you are 'marking up' the artwork for yourself then the registration marks must be made in ink and outside the page area. They are an extension of the imaginary line that determines the exact page size both horizontal and vertical. There will be two registration marks outside each of the four corners of your double page spread and there will be two vertical registration marks outside the page area indicating the middle, or gutter, of the spread. All of this information goes on the paper outside the page area.

FROM ROUGH TO ARTWORK

By the time one is ready to begin the artwork one has worked out the composition, decided on characters, the size and shape of the book and how to tell the story. There are fresh decisions to be made now and the first is how to get the rough drawing onto a quality paper so that it can be coloured. Nowadays many illustrators scan images into their computers and work on them this way, negating the need for materials or quality papers, and this is one way of working.

Using quality materials, papers with a particular surface or texture, favourite inks or special colours can add a great deal to the eventual success of the artwork. Also the very act of creating an image this way, with real materials, knowing that it can be easily ruined with a careless action, adds a certain frisson to making illustration that is difficult to get any other way. One works all day drawing and inking in an illustration from a rough onto a piece of quality paper, then comes the moment when one adds the paint. The choice of colour cannot easily be altered if it is ink or watercolour, as this relies on the whiteness of the paper shining through to give the colour brilliance. The tension of this moment can add an excitement and freshness to illustration that should not be underestimated.

Usually when one works on the rough drawings, and they go well, there is a liveliness to them. Keeping this same liveliness in the artwork can be difficult and in a way it is often this that dictates how one gets from rough to artwork.

If you are the kind of illustrator who produces a very careful, thorough rough then the simplest way to get it onto good quality paper is to use a light box. If the paper is thin enough to be

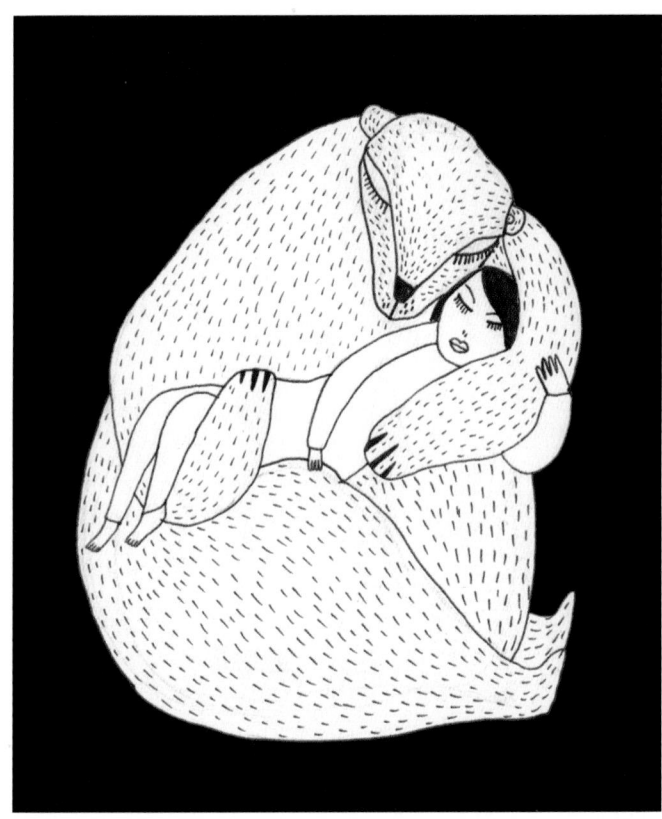

Rina Donnersmarck manages to imbue these two characters of the girl and the bear with real feeling. Look especially at the way each holds the other. It is this that makes this illustration such a tender and gentle image.

put on the light box and still show the rough underneath then it can be simply and lightly traced onto the paper. I like to trace my rough onto tracing paper as a mirror image and then transfer it onto quality paper by turning it over and rubbing the back of the tracing. This is primarily because I like to use paper of a very heavy weight, so that it does not wrinkle when I put washes on, and my rough drawing cannot be seen through the paper, even on the light box. But also I like the fact that by using this method, I can reposition the drawing on the paper and this gives me the opportunity to change the angle at which we view the drawing.

If you do not have a light box then you can trace the drawing by holding it up against a window. This works in exactly the same way but can be a little awkward especially if the illustration is large.

Many illustrators do not like to trace the rough at all but prefer to copy the drawing onto their paper. It takes great skill to produce an identical drawing freehand and, of course, it probably will not be identical. It will be a different drawing. Depending on how good you are at this the differences may be subtle or vast but differences there will be and it is these differences that can turn a lively rough into static artwork or, if you are clever, or maybe just lucky, into a drawing that is equally fresh and full of life.

Another way of keeping the immediacy of a rough through to artwork is not to draw them again at all but instead to photo-copy the roughs onto the best paper you can get to go through your machine. Depending on how you use the tonal control you may have a line as light or as dark as you wish whilst still keeping the freshness of the original rough. The main difficulty with this method is getting a good enough quality paper to go through the photocopier without jamming it up. Also it is worth remembering that many copier inks, especially if you are

In these illustrations by Lynn Hatzius, from her new picture book, *On the Magic of Smiles*, (*Vom Zauber des Lachelns*) Lynn uses collage to stunning effect here and these illustrations brim with atmosphere and feeling. This is a book in the making and even at this stage Lynn is still playing with composition and colour. It is possible these illustrations may yet change several times before Lynn is absolutely satisfied.

THE FINISHED ILLUSTRATIONS

using the computer, are not waterproof and so can 'pick up' if you are using watercolour over the top.

To return to the practice of scanning in images to then work and develop on a computer, clearly you would expect that a lot of the freshness would remain. After all, it is the same drawing. It is strange then that, often, the very problem with computer-generated artwork is that it can look lifeless.

It is unlikely that every piece of artwork you produce will turn out exactly as you hope. In a 32-page book there are usually a couple of spreads that just will not go right! Try not to get stuck on these, endlessly reworking a particular spread again and again, but work on through the rest and revisit them at the end. You may see it differently by then. What you thought was not good, after time, may appear perfectly fine. Alternatively, it may be necessary to return to the roughs and completely rethink the entire page.

Whether you work on the spreads in the order they appear in the book or whether you work on them in order of preference is up to you of course. Working in chronological order has the advantage of making sure that the continuity is correct and you are much less likely to make mistakes of this nature. However, working on your favourites first has the advantage that if they turn out as well as you are expecting then that might give you the encouragement to press on with the book. Illustrating a picture book, as we discussed earlier, is a very big project, and sustaining it through to the end takes a very great deal of commitment and motivation.

Some illustrators like to first draw out all of the artwork for the complete book before then colouring all of the artwork. This is practical and probably saves time, if that is at a premium. This also takes a deal of self-belief. Personally, I need to see that the book is working and turning out well by seeing how the artwork is looking. It is this that encourages me to continue with the rest of the illustrations.

It can take a few spreads to get into the swing of the book. Many illustrators come back to the spreads they began with to rework them at the end of the book because somehow they no longer seem to fit with the main body of work – it has changed

and evolved as the artwork has been completed. The thing is to try and enjoy this part of the book and not feel pressured or inhibited. Like all the other stages of making a children's book nothing is set in stone. Even at this stage you might still want to completely rethink how the book will look and that is absolutely fine.

LOOKING AGAIN AT THE COMPOSITION

Of course we have already spent a lot of time talking about composition in the earlier chapters so, ideally, by the time we are working on the artwork the composition should be decided. However, it may be a good idea at this stage to cut a window mount (a piece of white paper or card with a whole cut out of the centre to the page size that you are working to). If you have been fairly generous with your bleed, move the mount over your artwork, framing and re-framing your illustration with alternative compositions. Move the mount down, cropping the top. Try pulling the mount to one side, off-setting your original composition. This is an excellent way of seeing your illustration afresh, surprising yourself with compositions you might never have thought of.

PROJECT NINETEEN:
OUTSIDE INFLUENCE

Looking at other illustrators' work, finding inspiration and learning by looking at how others make illustration is an essential part of personal development as an illustrator. Try to make an effort to see real artwork by visiting exhibitions and galleries. Many cities have art galleries where one can see the work of illustrators. Some even have museums or galleries devoted just to illustration. Nothing usually beats the experience of looking at a piece of real artwork because here you can see exactly how the image has been created.

Libraries offer another opportunity to study the work of fellow illustrators and of course there is the Internet. It is all food for the creative mind and time spent looking at what is going on in your field is time well spent.

PROJECT TWENTY:
DRAWING FROM MEMORY

As has been previously discussed, keeping the life in your artwork is a challenge. The best way to keep the life in a drawing is to draw it as much as possible quickly and freely trying not to worry exactly how it will turn out. Confidence is a great help. Take an illustration that you have worked up to rough state. Look at it carefully then put it aside. Try to redraw this image again without looking at it, do not get bogged down with redrawing or using an eraser; it does not matter how this turns out – it is only an exercise. By repeating this exercise with different illustrations you should find that your confidence builds and that when the time comes to transfer a drawing, you will not feel intimidated.

PROJECT TWENTY-ONE:
IN THE MIRROR AND UPSIDE DOWN

When working on the illustrations for a book for long periods of time it is difficult to 'see' them. One can end the day feeling dissatisfied with one's efforts or just not have a clear idea of whether the illustration is good, bad or indifferent. It is very easy to wreck an illustration at this point. One may feel that something is wrong but not know quite what and start changing various things in the illustration only to find it is now worse than before.

Try looking at work in the mirror. This is a way of seeing an illustration afresh. One can view it from a new standpoint. Looking at an illustration upside down gives the same opportunity to re-assess it.

Of course the best thing of all is to put the illustration in a drawer or face to the wall and look at it again the next morning. Looking at the illustration after a period of time is hugely beneficial and often one can see immediately where the problem lies or indeed if there was a problem at all.

When working professionally there is often not the time available for assessing one's own work in this way, which is a pity. It is very often the case that one might rework an entire illustration only to return to one's first attempt at the end, noticing that actually it was not half as bad as you had thought!

Some fly long distances,

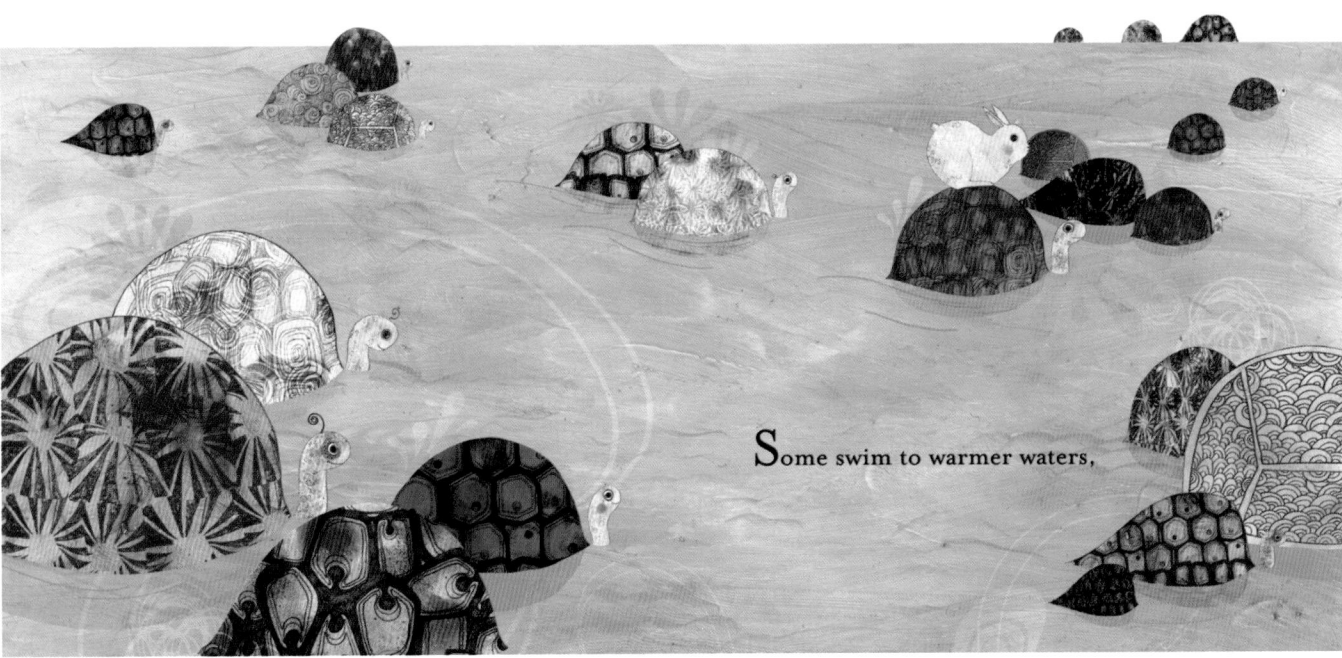

Some swim to warmer waters,

These four beautiful spreads are from Il Sung Na's *Brrr: A Book of Winter* and they sing with colour and pattern. Although the book is about winter and how the characters cope with it, Il Sung uses quite warm colours alongside the blues and whites so that when we read that the sheep cope with winter by having thick fleecy coats, despite the fact that it is snowing, they do actually look warm. Il Sung achieves a similar feeling with the ducks that are flying off to a warmer place.

While some have
a thick, cosy coat...

...they can stay
in the snow!

Some stay very still,

PROFILE:
CLARE BEATON

Clare Beaton has worked as an illustrator for over thirty-five years, illustrating over a hundred books for children, many with an interactive element to them.

When working on my books I find roughs are the most difficult but also the part I like best because it is drawing, which I do not do with the artwork. The roughs are the only time I actually use pen and pencil. I will not be able to change the design of the books after the roughs because of the text so it is here that I sort the book out. The publisher always wants the roughs to be busier, which is not always my preference.

By the time I come to make the artwork I know what I am doing. I work using fabrics, felts and collage. I like old things but hate the word 'vintage' and the reprinting of retro-fabrics, which rather undermines the point of vintage. I have favourite fabrics, of course, and old aprons are an especially great source for materials, I use every scrap – they have such lovely details.

I do not like to work in chronological order. I do not want the book tailing off and if I find a fabric I like I do not really want it on consecutive spreads. Also my mood might change whilst on the lengthy task of completing the book. If I work on the spreads in a random order this is far less likely to be apparent.

Even though I have sorted out the book with the roughs there are still lots of decisions to be made regarding the artwork. I have to choose which fabric, colour, pattern, and shape, and all of this can take ages. Then there is the cover which is usually the most difficult to produce because it is so important. I might do the cover rough fourteen times or so before taking it to artwork.

I have a good working relationship with my publishers. I have worked with them a long time and trust them, usually finding that comments as to alterations nearly always work out for the best. Having said that, they like me not to be adventurous which I mind and find constricting. It is easy to feel typecast but I think many illustrators feel this. The publishers need to know what they are going to get whereas the illustrator is eager to break new ground. I find I cannot change my style because the publisher wants what I do.

I always wanted to be an illustrator; drawing was my top thing. I studied at Hornsey Art School which I loved, in fact I made myself ill working so hard. Art School was a great grounding. I have no preferred time for work and can work anytime. I now have my own studio where I can leave everything out but, even when I did not, I made a space. Radio 4 is on all day long and I find this is great to work to.

Naïve art or folk art is the thing I like best: I like the quirkiness of it and the idea of being untrained although, as I have said, I loved my time at Art School. I have yet to produce an entire book that I like, the odd page perhaps and I often think, if only I could revisit a publication... the life of an illustrator!

Clare Beaton.

These three double-page spreads are from Clare Beaton's *Bedtime Rhymes*. She has made the illustrations using a felt and fabric collage. Her use of a limited palette is particularly effective in creating mood and atmosphere.

If you have managed to write and illustrate your own children's picture book then that is a huge achievement and one can feel justifiably proud of the motivation, commitment and serious hard work that will have gone into this process. This might well be enough for you.

Nowadays small editions of one's own book can be easily printed and copied and distributed to friends. In fact there has never been a better time to do just this. The Internet has made this task simple and relatively cheap. However, if you are looking to cast your book at a larger audience then perhaps you are hoping to find a professional publisher to publish it. This task is far from easy, but there is a good way to go about it.

WHOM TO APPROACH?

Most publishers have a preference for certain kinds of book. One can easily find out what this is by looking at the publisher's list. Visiting a bookshop and looking in the children's books section will give you an idea of who publishes what and whether or not your book would fit in with that company. Some publishers will only publish a very small number of children's books each year. Some will only publish books of a certain kind, for example, activity books or novelty books or books for very young children. It helps to find out about all of this before you start approaching all and sundry. Having your book continual-

ly turned down is demoralizing and expensive. A little research beforehand could save you a fortune and some unhappy hours. It used to be much easier to telephone the children's editor, arrange an appointment and visit them with your book. But increasingly the response to a telephone call, assuming one can even get through, is to send some copies or spreads from your book and, if these meet with a favourable reception, an appointment might then be arranged. The trouble with this is that it is very one-sided. What does the illustrator get from this arrangement if the reception is not positive? There is usually no feedback other than a cursory standard note, therefore it is impossible to know on what grounds the book is not suitable. It may be something that one would be willing and able to rectify or it may be a case of re-working the book in a fairly major way (which one may or may not wish to do), or it may be a case of calling it a day – the book is so unsuitable that it will never find a publisher. The trouble is one has no idea which.

I do also believe that meeting an editor face to face is of benefit to both. Part of a successful picture book is the collaboration of the people who go about making it happen and discussing these ideas and getting to know people is very much part of this process.

There are still publishing houses where you can arrange a visit first off but they are increasingly few, so if sending a few spreads is all that is available then, do not send too much. One is trying to arrange a visit so there should be a purpose to it, like seeing the rest of the book. The spreads sent are to whet the appetite.

Girl and Chicken by Rina Donnersmarck.

WHAT TO TAKE?

When visiting a publishing house with a picture book that you want them to publish you should have the story typed out so it is easy to read, the rough dummy book and a few of the spreads to artwork. Four double spreads are ideal.

You may think that your book would be more appealing if you finished it and included all of the spreads as finished artwork. However you would be mistaken: the publisher will want to be involved with your book. They will want to influence it and discuss possibilities and make their own suggestions as to how it evolves. If you hand them a *fait accompli* then where is the interest for them? Again one is hoping to excite and tempt, not dictate.

It is usual to make colour copies of the four finished spreads and stick these into the dummy book where they appear in the story, the black and white roughs forming the rest of the dummy. If you have drawn directly in the dummy then do not do this but present them as separate spreads. Likewise, the story should be written or typed out and stuck into the dummy, as you want it to appear on the spreads.

If you have worked digitally then print the spreads out. If you have worked with media then take the artwork – there is no substitute for seeing the real thing – and drop a white window mount over it, showing the page area as it will appear in the book. Hinge this at the top by folding it over and lightly tack it to the back using masking tape so that it can be lifted to show the bleed edge of the artwork, if there is one. Never cut artwork out and never use a coloured mount.

ATTITUDE

If you are offering your book for publication then it is worth bearing in mind that you are asking a publishing house to invest money, a great deal of money, in your book. If they do not like your book and feel that it would not be a worthwhile enterprise then there is no point resenting this and getting cross. You have asked for their opinion and they have given it. Furthermore it is reasonable to assume that you are receiving advice founded on years of experience and successful practice.

You are free to try elsewhere where opinion may be different but unless you are very lucky or very clever you will probably find that after a time similar comments are made again and again. It is worth taking these on board. Everyone has heard the stories of best selling, record breaking books that become publishing phenomena having previously been turned down by almost every publisher, but I suspect that this is a rare thing. I worked with an excellent children's book editor who had read

A 'Baddie' by Rina Donnersmarck.

The first task is a very important morning meeting.

A double-page spread from Sarah Dyer's *Monster Day at Work*.

and turned down *Watership Down* by Richard Adams. It is worth adding that she never liked the book even after its great success – we do not all like the same things. If one is repeatedly being given the same advice then it seems only sensible to act on it. It is sometimes difficult to see one's own work objectively when one has been so close to it for many weeks. A fresh eye may be just what is needed.

To put the other side of this argument, if one is going to become involved in making endless changes to a picture book proposal then I think it is only reasonable to ask for some commitment on the part of the publisher. If an initial response is that, it is felt, the book would be improved by a different palette or the rethink of a character, then that is fine. This is made as a helpful suggestion and it is up to you whether you act on this or not. Let us say that you do and return with the revised proposal and now the feedback is that the book needs a greater variation in backgrounds. Well okay, but this might go on and on with the end result being that there is still no intention of publishing your book.

So, in summary, listening to and perhaps acting on advice is common sense. To get embroiled in the endless tinkering of your book without any commitment or remuneration on the part of the publisher is best avoided. It is not unreasonable to expect some financial commitment, even a very small one, for complex and lengthy alterations. If nothing more, it shows that the interest is serious and not just kind words.

MORE THAN ONE IDEA

If you are going to go to the trouble of visiting a publishing house with your dummy book, story, and four finished spreads of artwork, then it is a good idea to have some other ideas for books. It is possible that, if interested in your style, a publisher, whilst believing the particular book you offer is not right for them, might well be tempted with something else. These 'other' ideas do not have to be worked up to dummy and spreads, but might be presented as roughs and visuals, character studies and a story outline. Again, remember that you are trying to tempt the editor with your ideas here; the more seductive and exciting the visuals the more chance you have of engaging interest.

Working on roughs and back-up sketches and presenting these in a lively way, your ideas for a book visualized in fact, can often be successful where finished artwork and a dummy are not. It is again this thing of a picture book being a two-way creation between publisher and illustrator. Offered the chance to be in on a book in the early stages where almost anything remains possible is an exciting prospect. A picture book worked

on in this way may well turn into a book that neither party had envisaged exactly at the beginning.

WORKING ON SOMEONE ELSE'S STORY

The author illustrator is a rare thing and most children's illustrators illustrate other writers' stories not their own. It is possible that having taken in your picture book and offered it for publication the response has been, 'It is not quite right, but what about having a go at illustrating this story?' and a story is handed over by an established writer.

This is a different challenge and the first thing to establish is exactly what is expected and what the remuneration might be. If there is to be no remuneration then you clearly have to calculate how serious the offer is. What is to stop the editor asking fifty illustrators to ' have a go' at this story? If there is not going to be a financial outlay then surely the more illustrators that are asked, the greater the choice for the publisher to choose from. Your chances of securing the commission are rapidly diminishing. In reality it is more usual for three or four illustrators to be offered the same book. They are asked to produce a sample spread, the choice of which is sometimes dictated by the editor, in which case all of the illustrators are usually asked to sample the same spread, and sometimes it is left up to the illustrator. Sometimes there is more than one book on offer, although it is still usual for all of the illustrators to sample the same spread. A rejection fee is usually offered for this work. This is a nominal sum that will be paid for the work if you are unsuccessful in obtaining the commission. If you are successful then obviously a contract will usually follow.

THE SAMPLE SPREAD

Producing a sample spread is a very difficult thing. For a start there usually is not very long in which to supply it, perhaps a week or two if one is lucky. This obviously means that all of the usual background work and research, character development and thinking yourself into the book cannot happen. It also means that everything is dependent on your producing one stunning spread.

Personally, I find that when working on picture books I often ditch the first spreads I have produced and do them again, because by the time I get to the end of the book, not only have I found the tempo, but I have often changed my mind from my starting point so that the initial spreads look less confident and

This is a sample illustration for *The Labours of Hercules*, this being the task of slaying the Erymanthian boar. In the end I decided to render these illustrations as wood engravings, not pen and wash as here. The shiny and smooth Fabriano paper gives this image a fresh and lively feel.

These character drawings from a book by Julia Donaldson called *The Trial of Will Wolf* were requested from the publisher to give them an idea whether or not I would be suited to this book. As you can see from their comments, they thought this, the central character Will, too scary – one of the editors has written that he looks mad! The story is a re-telling of Little Red Riding Hood with a twist; this character in the story represents the wolf, Will. I did indeed secure this commission although when all of the artwork had been finished the decision was made, at an editors' meeting, that Will should in fact appear as a wolf not as a human character. This meant quite considerable alterations to the artwork!

do not seem to fit. With a sample it is unlikely I am going to have the time to explore the spreads in this way – the first double spread I produce will have to get me the book!

It is a good idea to throw oneself into the business of producing a sample spread as if one had already been asked to illustrate the book, time permitting. If a specific double spread has been asked for, then one is obliged to produce it. However, all of the roughs and character sketches that you might have found the time to do are also worth presenting. These show how your mind is reacting to the book and are more appropriate than the spread. If you have the time, try several of the spreads out. One will just have to accept that one is not being paid for this work but then, if you secure the commission you will not care, and if you do not secure it, then you can feel you gave it your best shot.

Often, when one is asked to produce a sample spread, it is with the attitude that one should not go to too much trouble: 'Have a go!' or, 'Could we see a few quick sketches?' If you want the book then it is worth every bit of effort to ensure you get it for, if it is decided that it is perhaps not the book for you, then it is a comfort to know that you could not have produced a better sample.

This is the sample spread, entitled 'Woolly Rhinoceros' that I produced for *The Ice Age Tracker's Guide* published by Frances Lincoln. As usual with these things the sample came before I had any of the reference and before the design of the book had been worked out. It was not certain how much text would go on this double page or in what style it would appear. There were possibilities to hand-render the text, to set it, or even to have as if it had been typed. I mention all of this because it was quite clear that if I got to secure the book then I would almost certainly end up re-doing this sample spread.

The author of this book, Professor Adrian Lister, is also Research Leader in Palaeontology at the Natural History Museum in London and he arranged for me to visit the museum early in the morning before it opened so that I could draw from the exhibits and have the entire museum to myself. Having drawn from a real woolly rhinoceros skeleton, I did indeed re-draw this animal for the final artwork, correcting the many inaccuracies that I made in my sample illustration.

GETTING AN AGENT

Many illustrators have agents, therefore a lot of the activities mentioned in this chapter – showing your work around, visiting publishing houses, knowing whom to visit and what to take – will not be your worry but your agent's. It is often harder to secure a good agent than to secure a book deal and is it really beneficial anyway?

REASONS AGAINST

It is a very good agent indeed who can keep you constantly in work. They will almost certainly be representing many illustrators with their agency. Their top priority will be getting the job for one of their illustrators, not getting the job necessarily for you.

The fees decided upon by publishing houses are very often fixed. There is little negotiating to be done. This is what they pay for a 32-page picture book and that is that.

The vast majority of publishing houses are fair and honest. Clearly they want a good deal for themselves that makes money, why not? They are putting a great deal of their own money in to realize the project. They are usually not trying to trick you or take unfair advantage of foreign rights.

Finding out the publishing houses that are the most likely ones for your book is not an impossible task. There is a publication called *The Writers' and Artists' Yearbook*, which lists the names, addresses and contact numbers of publishing houses. A visit to a bookshop is a good way to get experience of who publishes what kind of illustration.

Usually when one has worked with an editor and publishing house on a book, assuming it has gone well, it is likely that they will remember you and use you again. Even if one has an agent, they will very often call you up directly. It will be up to you to inform your agent that they have been in contact to commission you. The agent will still expect to receive their percentage – after all had they not initiated the original collaboration this would not have happened.

You will have to agree to pay your agent a percentage of the fee they secure for you. This can be anything from 10 to 35 per cent of the fee they secure you.

In today's world much illustration work is done via the computer. Jobs are discussed over the telephone or by email. Illustrations are scanned in and sent. There is little 'leg work' to be undertaken.

Meeting the editors and designers at publishing houses is part of being an illustrator. The collaboration with these people is essential in producing a book that everyone is happy with. There is no substitute for talking this over, face to face. A good working relationship with your publisher is rewarding and productive. It is also the chance to meet new people that share an interest in illustration, and make friends. This is an aspect of a freelance illustrator's life that goes some way to countering the long hours working alone.

REASONS FOR

One can imagine that having an agent would enable you to be able to sit at home in your studio whilst wonderful choice commissions pour onto your desk; what could be finer?

There would be no uncertainty or awkwardness in negotiating a good fee as your agent would do that and secure you the best deal possible.

Copyright issues, royalties and rights, which can be complex and difficult to grasp, would not be a worry. Your agent's experience would be very valuable here in spotting anything untoward.

A good agent is well connected with lots of contacts. They know who publishes what and are therefore in a good position to take your book to the most favourable publishing houses. Moreover, agents spend much of their time in publishing houses so are often on the spot when texts come in ready to suggest that you are just the person to illustrate that book.

An agent, in doing all of the 'leg work', saves you much expense in travelling costs and lengthy journeys. You have no need to live within travelling distance of cities, so a remote retreat or even another country is perfectly possible. You can be as shy and as retiring as you like. There is no need to meet anyone, as your agent will do that for you. No more awkward meetings, or having to hear an editor tell you that this work does not fit.

So maybe, in the end, it comes down to personal preference. Many illustrators do other things in order to earn a living. Maybe they lecture or have some other part-time or full-time job. Here an agent could be invaluable in saving time and being there to answer the telephone and deal with problems or just accept work, when you are unavailable.

This is a rough from *Reynard the Fox*, the chapter opening spread for the third chapter of the book I am currently working on. Bruin the bear has returned, the victim of one of Reynard's tricks, from an assignment undertaken for King Noble the lion. The idea behind this rough is that Bruin, usually strong and fearless, is reduced to a pitiful figure. The grandeur of the King's Hall and the emptiness of it, in comparison to the claustrophobia of the previous chapter, help emphasize the gap that exists between Reynard's world and that of the King.

PROJECT TWENTY-TWO:
A SAMPLE SPREAD

Find an existing story that would be suitable for a picture book. Better still ask a friend to choose one for you. A short fairy tale or maybe a news story from a local paper would be ideal. Now produce a sample spread for your chosen story. Obviously you will know that you are not going to have to then illustrate the whole story. Try to analyse if this makes a difference as to how you approach the story. Does knowing that this will be a 'one off' illustration change how you produce it?

Give yourself a time limit, one week or two as a maximum. This calls for great self-discipline, you may not suddenly award yourself more time if the week turns out busier than you expected. You must stick to what you agreed at the outset and by the time your deadline arrives whatever you have managed to produce will have to be it.

PROFILE: JUDITH ESCREET

Judith Escreet is the Art Director at the publishing house Frances Lincoln.

So much has changed over the last thirty years in publishing. There are many more really good children's picture books about. Psychologists and educators now understand the value of books for children from the earliest days and publishers have, of course, picked up on this. This means, however, that getting your book published is harder. Publishers are looking for something different in the writing and illustration – that little extra special twist or unique look that will make their book a winner.

I trained at what was the London College of Printing, now LCC, when Tom Eckersley was head of Graphic Design. I then went into a small design group, Kinneir Calvert, where I worked on all sorts of accounts and learnt a huge amount from the two partners. Margaret Calvert is an amazing typographer. I have always been an avid reader and love books and then decided I would like to move into publishing. I started off at Mitchell Beazley when Peter Kindersley was still Art Director. Then three of us from Mitchell Beazley set up a small packaging company working on children's books. And from there I went on to Walker Books when Sebastian Walker first set it up. At first we were working on non-fiction titles, but we soon branched out into picture books and I have been working in that area ever since.

Finding a great idea from an illustrator and working with them and the editor developing the idea and making it work as a book is the part of my work I enjoy most. So that's the initial stages from early concept through to the roughs and the final artwork. I guess that's the whole book that I enjoy working on.

Generally speaking, illustrators do not have a great deal of knowledge about publishing a book when they visit us with proposals. Those straight out of college tend to have ideas that are not fully formed or thought through carefully enough. But of course part of the joy of being at Art College is that you can experiment, so as Art Director I need to be able to see through the core of the idea and to help

make the project work. The computer and digital publishing mean that people feel they can do it themselves and don't understand that books for children are specialist things requiring a lot of skill and understanding on the part of all the people involved in the production of the book. Illustrators bring projects in at different stages of development. It can be a relief to see a project that is almost perfect. But there will always be some input needed from the publisher – the format of the book, the paper used, the binding and finishes, as well as inevitably, tweaking to the text and artwork.

It is important that proposals for books go down well at Bologna and Frankfurt, the two big book fairs. Publishing in the UK is mostly based on co-editions. It is hard work selling books and on the children's side an average print run in the UK is around 1,500–2,000 copies. It is important that all of the sales team back a book and feel that they can sell it in all markets. If the reception of a project is muted after a book fair then we would certainly need to reconsider the project, unless UK sales felt it was particularly suited to their market and was going to sell lots. But we tend to have considered the project and made a decision about it before we take it to a fair. It is now rare to get a definite sale at a book fair, whereas ten years ago many co-edition sales were made at Frankfurt and Bologna. People are far more cautious these days and need to consult their sales teams in detail. The whole process of selling co-editions is slower and quite often we won't make a sale in Europe until the book is printed.

There are occasions when I see a book and love it but I know that we won't be able to sell enough copies either in the UK or US. It might be because the subject is just not right for us, or that the project is too expensive to produce, or even that we simply can't afford the advance! I might then suggest another publisher.

The large book chains like Waterstones and W H Smith have a huge impact on what is published. They are able to command greater discounts from publishers and they only stock sure-fire sellers, which means that it is hard to get new authors and illustrators into these stores. Independent book shops find it extremely difficult to compete. But there are local branches of the chains that have managers who are dedicated to children's books and set up events with authors and illustrators and get behind books.

Although it is usually an adult who will buy a picture book, the child is always central to the book. It's important that the editors and designers are aware of what is happening in schools and libraries and understand what children like and need as part of their development. The cover can be the one thing that is aimed at the buyer – an adult – but it must still have child appeal.

On the whole we get more text submissions than author/illustrator submissions and it can be quite hard finding the right illustrator to go with a text. We might have a text for a couple of years before the right illustrator comes along. But it is still hard finding original, lively picture books.

I think it is very important that an Art Director or designer does get on with the illustrator. Not everyone likes exactly the same things and I think that it is possible that I might be working with an illustrator whose style I do not personally like. I might still feel that the book is commercial and other people in the team may like it. It's then important to make sure the illustrator does not know this. It is more of a challenge putting the book together and still very worthwhile. Children are capable of dealing with difficult subjects and ideas but I do think often adults tend to shield them and think that they can't cope. Interestingly, European publishers tend to be braver and publish much more challenging books than in the UK. Recently there has been a spate of books on death and one of the most moving and successful is *A Monster Calls* by Patrick Ness, illustrated by Jim Kay. It tackles the very difficult subject of a boy coming to terms with the fact that his mother is dying of cancer. This is an older fiction title but there have been picture books on that subject as well. One that we looked at buying in is *Duck, Death and Tulip* by Wolf Erlbruch, published by Gecko Press, about a duck making friends with death. In the end we decided it was too sophisticated and bleak for us to publish. In picture books it is important that there is some sort of resolution and an ending that leaves the child feeling satisfied and not distressed, whilst still stimulating them.

My advice to illustrators wanting to publish a book would be to make sure that you have thought the whole story through and that the story has a beginning, a middle, and an end. Rough it all out – that can be a small story board rather than full-sized roughs. Also do some artwork in colour, maybe just one or two pieces showing the main characters. Bring a portfolio of your work but don't restrict it to just one style. There have been so many occasions when an illustrator has shown me a project with a particular style of artwork and when I have looked at the portfolio I have seen something else that I think would work better. Make sure that you research the publishers that you want to approach. If it is a baby book, make sure they publish at that level. If it is going to be an older picture book make sure that it fits in with their list. And the most important thing of all is to draw, draw, draw. Even with all the work that is done on the computer it is still vital that your work shows that you have this ability. Thinking of all the great illustrators, they all have drawing as the basis of their work.

I am often asked if I have a favourite children's book. I love John Burningham's books and one of my favourites is *The Shopping Basket*. I think John has a wonderful mixture of child sensibility and anarchy. Just what children love.

Judith Escreet.

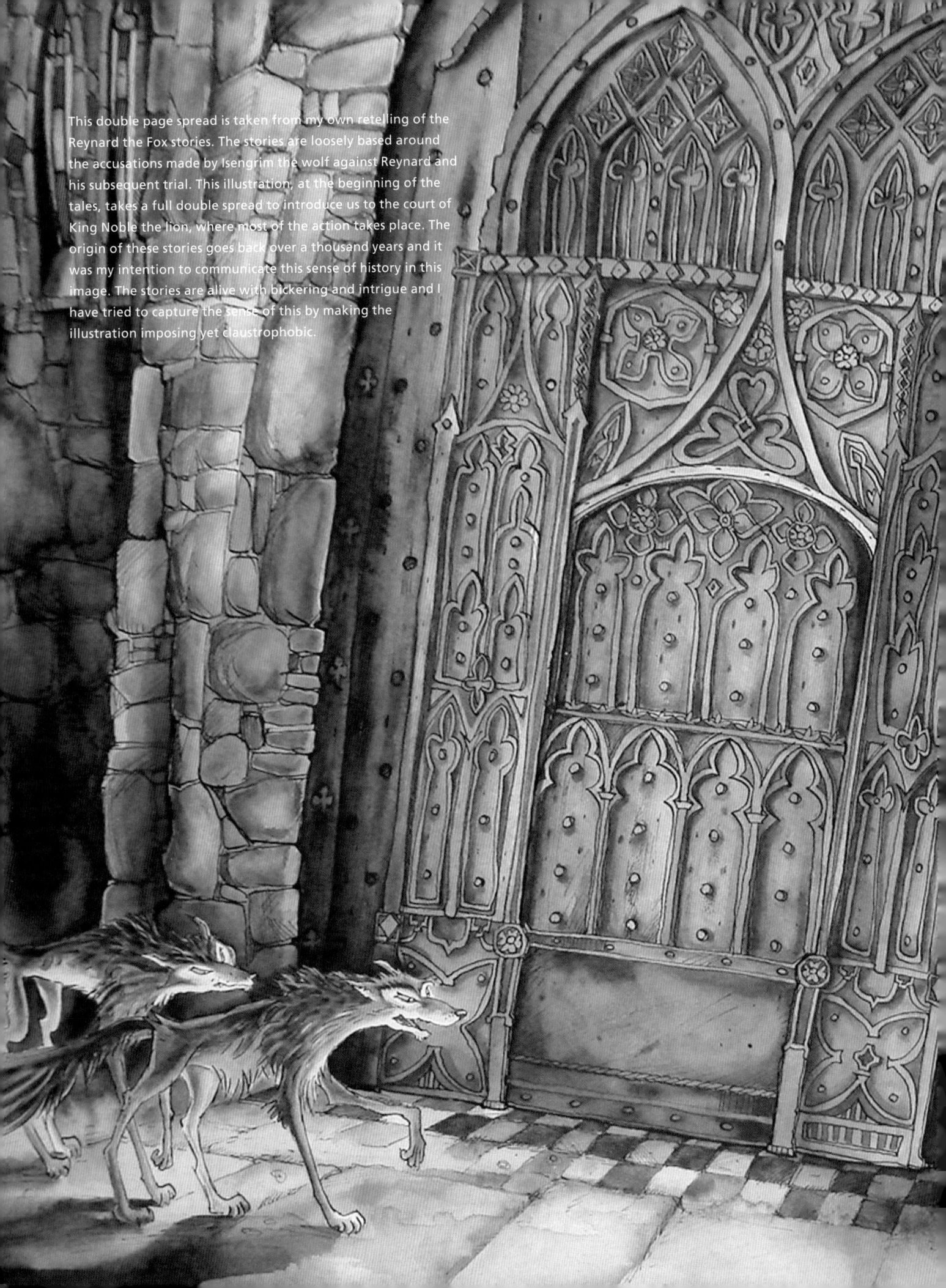

This double page spread is taken from my own retelling of the Reynard the Fox stories. The stories are loosely based around the accusations made by Isengrim the wolf against Reynard and his subsequent trial. This illustration, at the beginning of the tales, takes a full double spread to introduce us to the court of King Noble the lion, where most of the action takes place. The origin of these stories goes back over a thousand years and it was my intention to communicate this sense of history in this image. The stories are alive with bickering and intrigue and I have tried to capture the sense of this by making the illustration imposing yet claustrophobic.

Chapter Nine
LONGER STORIES

The main content of this book has been to do with the business of illustrating and perhaps writing your own children's picture book and, as has been discussed, these are nearly always 32-page picture books. However, it may be that you are interested in illustrating a longer book, maybe working on an out-of-print text or writing your own children's novel aimed at an older age range.

There is also a market for 'readers' – longer stories, still generously illustrated in colour and often 64 pages in length. These books are devised in the educational departments of publishing houses and aimed at helping children learn to read. They are often graded or banded in various sets depending on the scale of reading ability and come under a variety of trendy names: Bananas (of which there are blue, red and yellow bananas, depending on your prowess at reading), Big Cats, Cartwheels, Conkers, Jackdaws, and so on. They are a rich opportunity for illustrators wanting to produce colour illustration for longer stories as nearly all children's publishers produce books of this type.

Novels for children where the page count exceeds 64 pages are usually illustrated in black and white with only the jacket running to colour. Long gone are the days when colour illustrations would be inserted on high quality paper or, going further back, 'tipped in' once the book was printed and bound. Graphic novels (or more properly, comics) provide further opportunity for longer illustrated stories. The graphic novel market has grown rapidly over the last decade and straddles the difficult crossover area of books aimed at teenagers and adults. This has traditionally been a very difficult type of book to publish. They are expensive to produce and the consumers of these books are a difficult and unpredictable audience to target. However, as has been said, this is an exciting and rapidly growing area in children's publishing.

BEGINNING A LONGER BOOK

Initially there is little difference in beginning the illustrations for a longer book. One still needs to produce visuals, go out with a sketchbook, develop characters through drawings and join all of this together as a sequence of finished roughs. If the book is to be a graphic novel/comic or reader then a dummy book would also be a natural progression for this sequence of activity.

With a longer story one is constantly thinking where in the book the illustrations should appear. One wants the illustrations to appear with the relevant text and also relatively evenly spaced in the book. It would not be very good if all the illustrations appeared at the end or in the middle. Also, when deciding which are the best parts to illustrate, one is looking to add something to the text, not to just illustrate what is already written.

SUSTAINING MOMENTUM

One of the main challenges in illustrating a longer book is sustaining interest not just for the reader but also for oneself in completing a lengthy and complex task. This is especially pertinent when working on a graphic novel, a project that may be many months, even years in duration.

It is important to ensure that the book does not tail off or become boring and dull; it should remain consistent and exciting. Look at varying your scale and using different angles and viewpoints to sustain interest but do not go mad as this is easily overdone (rather like receiving a letter from someone new to a computer and its myriad of typefaces who manages to incorporate a fair number of the more decorative fonts in a single missive); it should feel natural. Keeping the narrative moving and flowing is essential – one should always want to turn the page.

The preparation when illustrating longer stories needs to be thorough and fully thought through. It is no good half way through a graphic novel suddenly wishing you had made your character taller or given him a different hairstyle. Again, consistency is the key.

Every illustrator finds his or her own way of working; what works for you is what matters, not how someone else thinks it should be done. There is a very great deal of self-discipline needed in projects of this kind. If one concerns oneself with a page at a time and sets out a realistic plan of what should be completed by when and sticks to it, the book will gradually appear. Choosing a book that one wants to do is part of it but try not to under-estimate the industry needed in completing a project of this magnitude; like running a marathon, you are in for the long haul and there will be plenty of moments when one feels that one's energy has run out. I think it is often the case that the most successful illustrators are not just those that are most creative but those that are motivated and self disciplined.

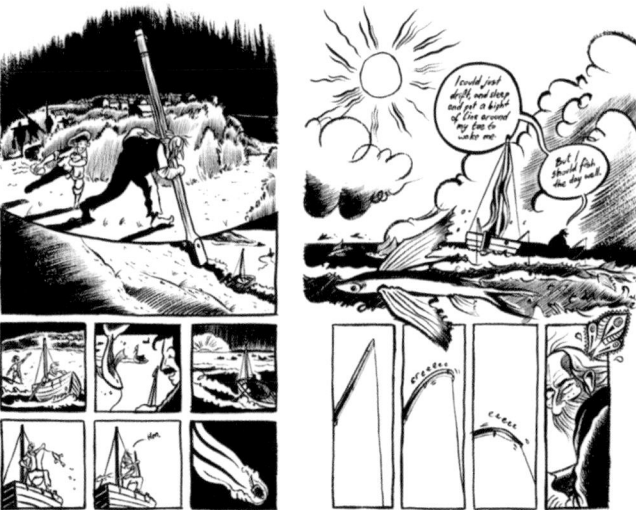

In these four double spreads for *The Old Man and the Sea* by the illustrator Corban Wilkin we can see how he has used a combination of exciting angles and dramatic view points in order to keep us fully engaged with the story.

The balance of black and white is excellent and we 'read' the images immediately. Corban is not afraid to leave white space and by not always drawing in the frame edge he helps increase the perception of scale in these pictures. The sea appears suitably vast. The absence of frame outlines in some of these captions also helps keep the narrative moving. His handwritten text complements the drawings perfectly and the two work in complete harmony creating a single image. Corban is drawing with a brush and ink and this has helped create the dramatic contrast in these thrilling images.

Here is the greater part of a set of pencil roughs from my own book, *Who Really Killed Cock Robin?* For this book I took as my starting point the old nursery rhyme and turned this into a murder mystery. The idea was that the clues in the illustrations enabled you, if you were observant, to work out who really killed Cock Robin. At the same time the book, which I researched for over six months, was full of the customs, superstitions, folklore, and traditions surrounding the ritual of death and burial from the medieval period until the mid-twentieth century. This is one of the most interesting projects I have worked on, a favourite.

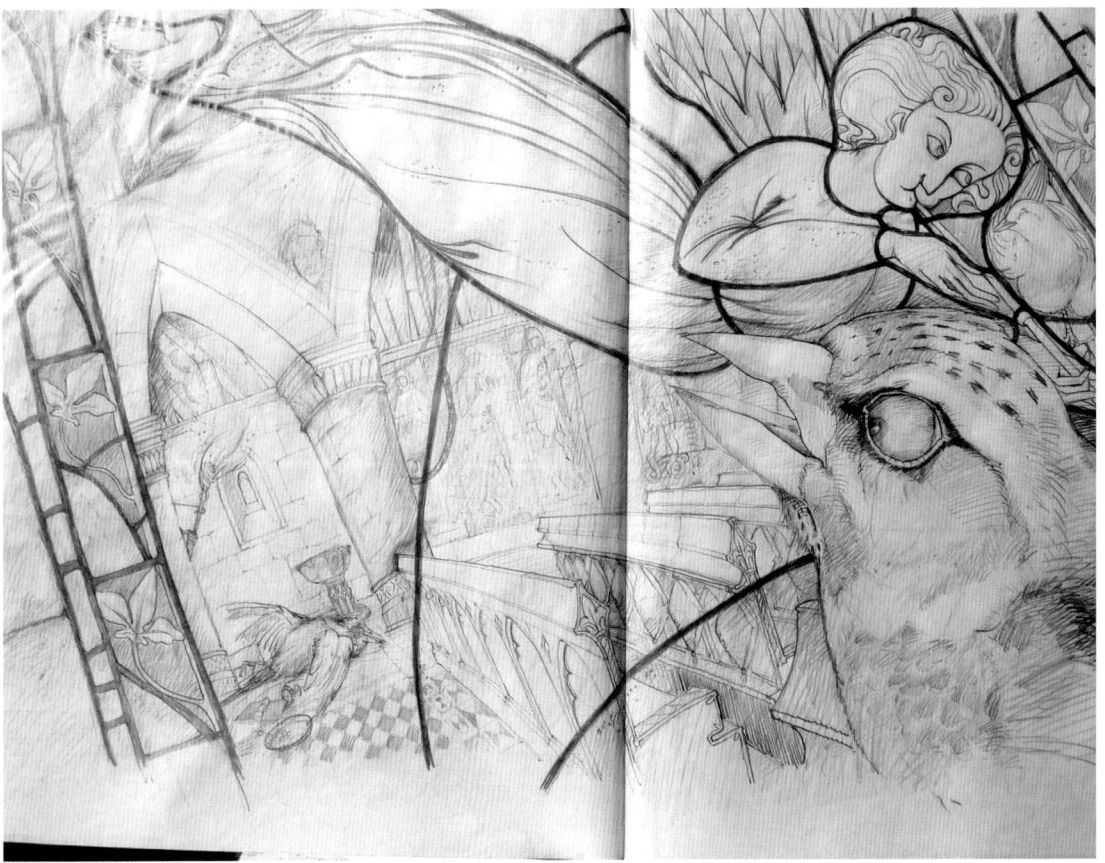

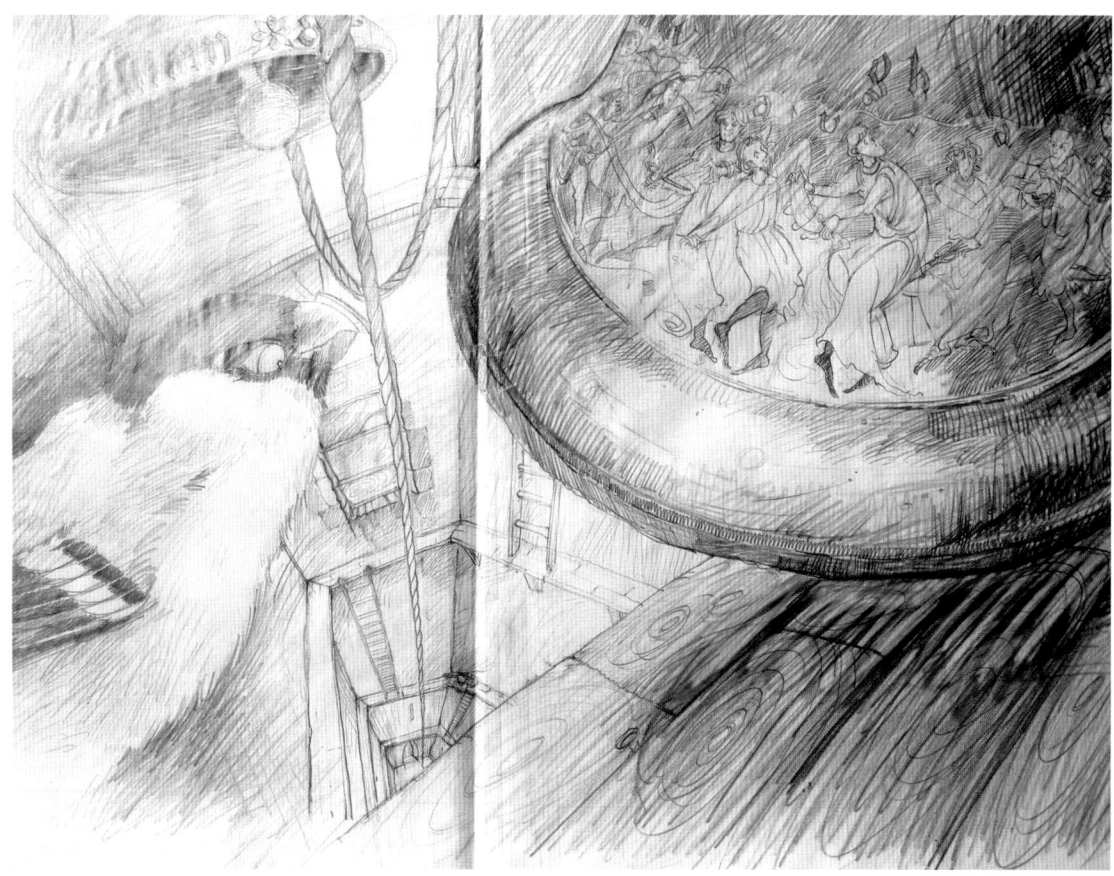

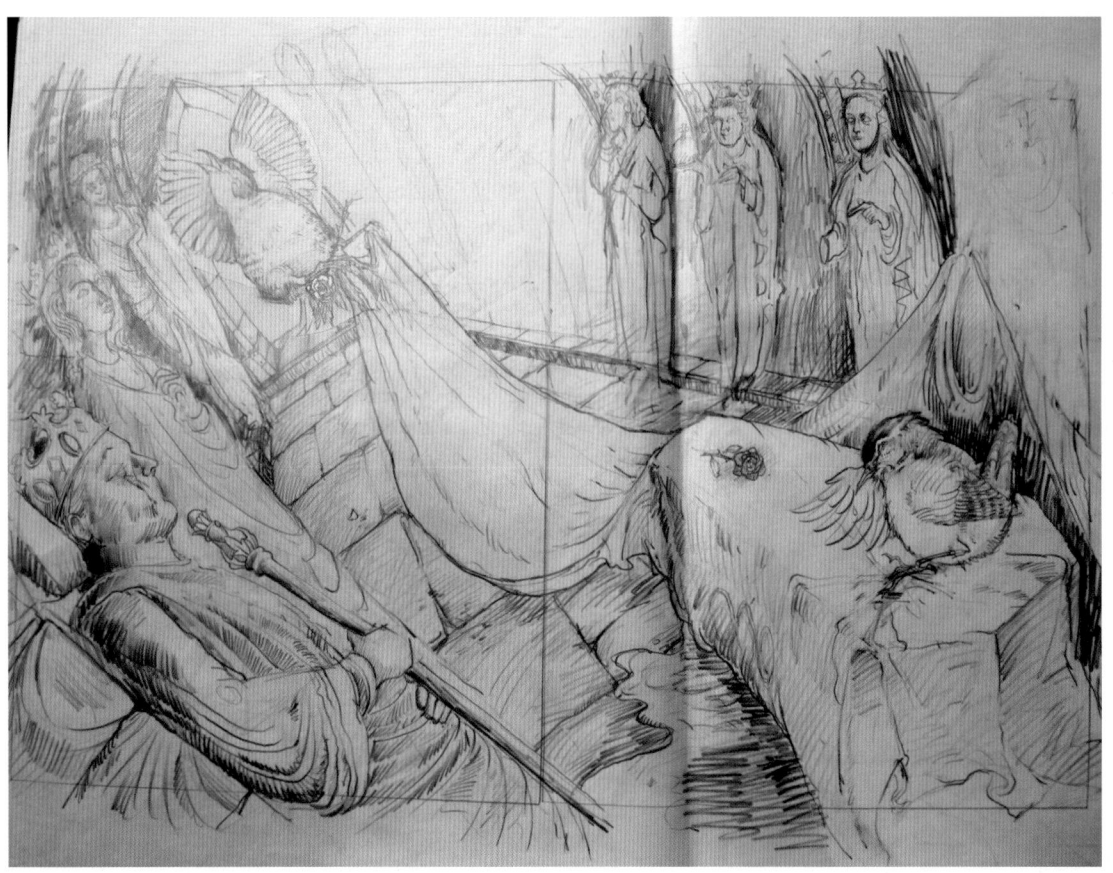

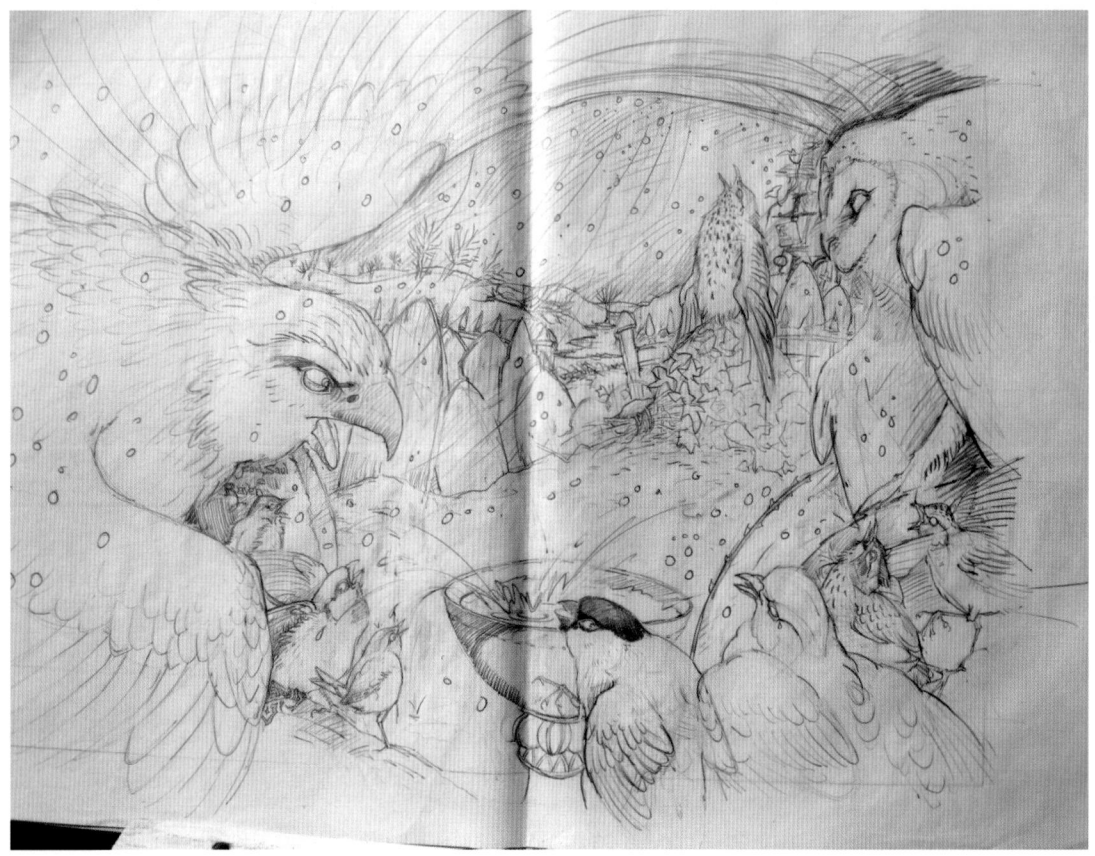

In this double-page spread from Corban Wilkin's *The Beauty of the Dead* we can see again how his hand-rendered text fits perfectly with the illustration. The speech bubbles do not look in the least crammed or crowded, they have plenty of room and have obviously been considered from the outset of this book.

It is worth adding that the composition of this double spread and the clever way in which these multiple frames work together to produce one illustration, is expertly achieved. These illustrations work both as individual images but also as a terrific double spread.

SPEECH BUBBLES IN GRAPHIC NOVELS

One of the main features of a graphic novel or comic book is the use of speech bubbles. Clearly, large areas of text within the illustration itself, usually set on a pale, if not white, background is going to drastically alter the design and visual impact of the image. Designing the illustrations with this in mind is crucial. Start with the text: it is always better to begin knowing how much room the text is going to take up as opposed to making a beautiful image and then trying to make the text fit. The text is always going to take up more room than you think.

Bear in mind that this text may need to be translated into other languages so always keep it on an overlay when producing the artwork.

Text can be hand rendered or set. Hand-rendered text can look great with drawn illustration, the text and image working together in perfect harmony. However, remember it has to be easy to read. Hand rendering the text is another skill and not a skill that every illustrator possesses. It needs to be neat and legible and again this should be done on an overlay.

GETTING THE MOST OUT OF THE ILLUSTRATIONS BUDGET

When supplying illustrations for a children's novel one is often commissioned to produce illustration by the page. The editor will take the text area as the size for a full-page illustration and commission the illustrator to produce, let us say, six pages of

A roughed spread from *Reynard the Fox.* I am working on this project at the time of this book going to press.

illustration. If the book is two hundred pages long, then six full-page illustrations will not seem very many in the context of the whole book, indeed one could flick through the pages and think the book is without any illustrations at all. However, if one decided to substitute the full-page illustrations for half-page illustrations, one would now have a two hundred-page book with twelve illustrations in it. One could divide the illustration size horizontally again so that we would have quarter-page illustrations; now there would be twenty-four illustrations in the book and although they would be small they might make very good illustrations to appear at the top of chapters or tail pieces for the ends of them. Certainly flicking through the pages of a two hundred-page book with twenty-four illustrations, one would realize at a glance that it was indeed illustrated.

The best way to get the most out of the illustrations budget for a book is to have a variety of full pages, half pages and quarter pages. How one divides up the quota is often left to the illustrator to decide and the fee will be the same whether one supplies six full-page illustrations or twenty-four quarter-page illustrations. It will certainly be quicker to produce six larger illustrations as opposed to twenty-four smaller, but what will make the more enjoyable book?

CONTINUITY

When working on longer stories there is usually more scope for time to pass within the story. The story may travel through months or years in time, unusual in the 32- page picture book. The characters may grow older and will almost certainly not remain in the same clothes throughout the book; therefore extra attention needs to given to making sure that the characters are easily recognizable and consistent. Hairstyle and colour, mannerisms, poses, facial features and idiosyncrasies are all useful in achieving this. Drawing directly from observation and recording these kinds of characteristics in your sketchbook is again of enormous benefit in making convincing illustration and avoiding generic imagery.

Working in chronological order, especially in graphic novels, is probably also a good idea, if not essential. Because the book is much longer it is more able to absorb imagery of a less dynamic nature. To go further, a book where the illustrations were relentlessly shouting all the way through would be a rather exhausting book to read and enjoy. The excitement and thrill of the story will be heightened by quieter passages.

PROJECT TWENTY-THREE: DIVIDING UP THE PAGE

Supply six pages of illustration for a novel you have read.
Read and re-read the novel, marking relevant passages that describe character and place. You will need to refer to these to make sure you get everything right. Make a list of the passages in the book that you wish to illustrate. Remember they should be more or less evenly spaced throughout the book and should be a combination of half-page, quarter-page and full-page illustrations. Choose more passages to illustrate than you need and work on these through roughs, selecting the most successful to work up to artwork.

When you have produced the finished artwork either scan the illustrations in or photocopy them and paste them with the text, as they might appear in the novel. You will get an idea of how setting the illustrations amongst the text can dramatically alter the illustration. Chapter headings can really help in creating the right atmosphere and in leading one in to read the story; likewise tailpieces help in bringing a conclusion to a chapter or in reinforcing a significant episode.

PROJECT TWENTY-FOUR: COMIC BOOK

Produce a short graphic novel.
Decide on your story and write it up. Text to go in speech bubbles should be set in the order it needs to be read. You will need to work out when working on the roughs how you intend to divide up the page. Remember that you will need the eye to read your frames in a particular order for the story to be coherent, so do not underestimate your reader's automatic adherence to a more conventional reading pattern. Where to go next when reading a graphic novel should not be a matter of guesswork.

Knowing how much space your text, including the text in speech bubbles, will occupy is worth establishing before beginning the roughs but when drawing the roughs do not leave a space where the speech bubbles go but draw behind them. The drawing will be more convincing if the speech bubbles are added on top, as opposed to stopping the drawing and picking it up on the other side of the text areas.

Try to keep your graphic novel short – perhaps five or six pages to start with. Even this is a big project and can take several weeks. When you have taken the roughs to artwork, copy and bind the book, either with a simple saddle stitch (staples) or sewn binding. Reading the book in this bound format helps one notice how the images read and how they work together on the page.

PROFILE:
CORBAN WILKIN

Corban Wilkin, winner of the Jonathan Cape Comica Graphic Short Story Prize 2012, has worked on several graphic novels including *The Old Man and the Sea* and *A Plague of Lighthouse-Keepers*.

When I am beginning a graphic novel, writing it is the most important part, working out the plot and the pacing of the story. Nothing can happen until I have done this. The real thinking stage is the thumbnails, and the finished artwork is the craft. By the time I get here nearly all of the decisions have been made. To put it another way, if the thumbnails are telling the story then the artwork is typing it out, I cannot be making it up at this point.

I have an ideas book where I constantly write down ideas, things I see or a news story, even stories by other people – it is not so much having an idea, more seeing an idea and developing it. Everyone has ideas but the success of it is what you do with it; it will not be 'gold' until you have worked on it and made something of it. To start with I think your idea has to be something that you are genuinely interested in. With a long project, three hundred pages plus, it is an advantage if you really want to do it. There may be a moment every day when one questions the point of pursuing the book. I do not know exactly what makes me sit at my desk, hoping to get better as an illustrator: a mad dedication to the act of creating something – who knows? I cannot imagine a situation where I am thinking I am good at this now – everything I do should add to my development as an illustrator.

I think the goal of publication, even self-publication (relatively easy now), is important in terms of motivation although the best bit of working on a graphic novel is the doing of it, the book coming out is the icing on the cake.

A longer book has a self-supporting structure; it can cope with less exciting parts to it. Also, one simplifies images more because the quantity works in its favour; for example, 'this' kind of image may not work on its own but does work very well as part of a set. If everything were made as complex images, different angles and viewpoints relentlessly through the book, one would wear the reader out. We are looking at the larger picture.

With a longer book I find one is more or less forced to work consecutively otherwise it would be easy to lose consistency. I sometimes work by taking a chapter at a time. Having worked out my characters it is important not to get into reassessing, for example, a different nose or hair style. Illustrators have their own individual style that is difficult to get away from but a book can change whilst one is working on it; it is important to watch this.

One of the challenges of the longer story is sustaining the reader's interest. I try to do this with visual variety, different perspective, close-ups and distant shots. Varying the images and sustaining conflict in the story is important. Creating characters that are trying to reach a goal that other characters frustrate is really just good story telling.

A big part of the graphic novel is text and image together. One can have sequences without text but the written story is an equal part. People who can draw cannot always write and one needs to be a storyteller. Just because it is 'graphic' the assumption is that one should give priority to the pictures. However, in a graphic novel like *Fun Home* by Alison Bechdel, where text and image work together in complete harmony, it is obvious that both are equally important.

I am not that bothered about the materials: I would draw with anything if it came to it. Having said that, I do like Sennelier Indian ink because it is so consistently black. Winsor and Newton series 7 brushes are great but expensive and I am quite fussy with which paper I use – so perhaps after all I am bothered!

My original inspiration was Chris Riddell. The skill of his line work is astonishing. The Canadian graphic artist Seth I also really like. His consistency and the quality of his drawing, which I think has an old fashioned sensibility, is an influence. However, my 'top influence' would have to be Craig Thompson. I love the looseness of the drawing, and he is such a great storyteller.

Corban Wilkin.

Cycling by Lynn Hatzius. In this lovely understated piece of collage, notice how effective the very restricted palette is in setting just the right feel to the illustration.

Four Christmas books by Martin Ursell. These A6 books are made by folding an A3 sheet in half three times, cutting and stitching it after printing (see Project 16). I usually send these books out each Christmas and they represent a thank-you for work commissioned throughout the year. They also act as an aide-memoire that I am working and available for more work and they are, of course, a vehicle for sending Christmas wishes.

It is a constant challenge to think of an interesting theme when working on printed ephemera of this kind, and never is this more difficult than when that theme is Christmas. What on earth can be thought of that has not already been illustrated to death? All I can say is that I do think this is worth the trouble and that with perseverance one can usually come up with something – even if some years will be more creative than others.

This book has been about illustrating children's books and the success of doing this does not depend on whether or not one manages to publish the book or then work as a professional illustrator. It is more than enough to have produced the illustrations for a story that you or someone else has written and you need feel no obligation to take this any further. Very often having committed to a project like this, and carried it through from initial idea to finished book, one is much better equipped to repeat the project with a new book. After all, one now knows what to expect and many of the difficulties that one may have successfully overcome may reappear in a new project, only now they can be tackled with the benefit of experience.

However, it is possible that, having produced your children's book and found a publisher to publish it, you might be eager, or even asked, to produce another book and maybe another after that. Therefore it might be useful to talk a little about how one keeps oneself going as an illustrator and what one can do to maximize the chances of keeping oneself in illustration work.

CREATING A WEBSITE

Setting up your own website is an excellent way of getting yourself known. Having a website means that prospective clients can look at your work without you going to visit them. Your work is readily available to see at the click of a mouse. It can be constantly updated and changed and one is not constrained by the limitations of what one can carry or fit in a portfolio. Also because one can view work on a website in any order it is easy to go straight to the relevant images as opposed to wading through an entire portfolio.

When setting up a website it is worth thinking about the design of it. What do you want people to see? It could have different sections, for example, one for published work, one for sketchbook work, maybe even a section for roughs. If you have worked on a successful picture book maybe you would like your readers to be able to see 'behind the scenes' of it: doodles and initial sketches, illustrations that did not go in the final book. You will probably want people to be able to contact you through your website, either by email or standard contact details (address, telephone, etc.). Perhaps you will also want to put on it a short biography saying what else you have done. One can buy website kits and create all this oneself or one can employ a designer; it is a matter of personal choice, although it is worth pointing out that a well-designed and smart website does create an excellent impression that is all the more likely to inspire confidence in a prospective client.

Of course none of this is of any use whatever if nobody looks at it so make sure prospective clients know it is there. A promotional postcard or printout that you might mail to publishing houses could awaken their curiosity, and may have the added advantage of finding itself tacked to a noticeboard where it would be a constant reminder of what you do.

Lastly, it is an idea once you have a website up and running to try and keep it fresh and updated so that regular visitors see something new each time they check it out. Imagine a shop window that did not change from one year to the next: after a while you would stop going in to look as one would assume they had nothing new to look at. A change to the loading page is especially pertinent as this is noticeable straight away.

BUSINESS CARDS AND PROMOTIONAL EPHEMERA

A business card with your contact details on is a good way of making sure editors and publishers can easily get in touch with you. A business card with an image on is better still. There they will have a constant reminder of who you are, what you do and how to contact you. Further to this, a card that is well liked may be put up in the editor's office, forming a constant aide memoire.

Many illustrators reproduce an illustration from something they have already had published to go on the card. This is fine as it may bring with it memories of the book it came from, but a fresh image that was not in the book may make a more attention-grabbing 'Post-it'.

Some illustrators produce a more individual business card, one that is hand-coloured, or even a hand-drawn and coloured image, therefore making each card an individual piece of artwork. Possibly this is less likely to be discarded, but it is a time-consuming and laborious process and is really only suitable for a small client list.

It is relatively easy to find professional postcard deals on the Internet where you can have 500 A6 postcards printed for a relatively cheap price. These can be scored and folded to make small business cards with multiple illustrated images or kept whole as postcards. Either way they are yet another useful way of getting your work seen and 'out there'.

Depending on the kind of illustration work you are hoping for, small print runs of zines and illustrated booklets given out on visits to publishing houses or mailed in excitingly illustrated envelopes are yet another way of drawing attention to your work and getting prospective clients to use you. Generating your own ephemera and promotional material all helps keep you in people's minds and it is difficult to overstate the effect self-promotional material can have on your workload. Personally illustrated Christmas cards to people you have seen or

worked with during the year, illustrated thank-you slips to follow up a visit, and compliments cards when you take work in, all help keep you in people's minds. I once received a considerable commission from an editor whose husband had been using an old illustrated compliments slip of mine as a bookmark; it must have been over ten years since I had last visited that publisher but the slip had provided a constant reminder.

GENERATING WORK

Whether one has commissioned work to do or not, it is very important to keep producing illustrations. By constantly working one is hopefully developing and getting better. Also, rather like a musician practising scales, if one stops drawing for any length of time one can very quickly get rusty and out of practice. Generating one's own projects and stories takes discipline, commitment and a great deal of self-motivation but it is the way to get better at being an illustrator.

The strange thing about all of this is that one would think that having lots of time in which to produce work would be an ideal situation whereas in reality it always seems to be easier to have ideas and produce new work whilst one is frantically busy. In other words the more work one does, the more work it is possible to do. I would go further and equate quality with this scenario: illustrators often produce their best work when they are working flat out and not when there is time to fiddle and rework ad infinitum.

Clearly there is a balance to be struck here: one does need time to 'see' what one has produced and this is really only possible after a short period of time has elapsed, but the fact

Baby in a Basket by Clare Beaton. Felt and fabric collage.

remains, I think, that one is much more able to work effectively if one is busy. The old saying holds true that creating something is ninety per cent perspiration and ten per cent inspiration.

It is not easy to keep working without specifically commissioned projects. Illustrators by their very nature enjoy and need the challenge of a brief and generating work that may have no professional outcome is very difficult to sustain. It might be far more tempting to spend the time in a garden or reading a book, but remember that as a freelance illustrator one needs to give oneself the best possible chance in an immensely difficult and competitive field and this does mean constantly producing new work.

There are plenty of ideas as to how to go about generating work in this book. Look at the suggested projects at the end of each chapter for inspiration and do not be afraid to develop or change the criteria of these projects to suit your own ends. By constantly producing new work one is continually updating and editing one's portfolio. This is not only essential for any illustrator in helping keep the work fresh and current but also a reason why a prospective client might continually watch out for what you are doing.

RECEIVING COMMISSIONS

One might be approached with a commission when one is frantically busy, or one might be approached when one has nothing on the go; either way, if at all possible, accept it and say 'yes'.

There are some provisos to saying 'yes'. Firstly, it should be at least possible to finish the commission by the set deadline. One should never be late with work and missing a deadline is certainly something to be avoided at all costs but, remember, you will almost certainly be working faster and more efficiently in the middle of the book as opposed to the beginning and it is amazing what can be achieved when the mind is focused. Working flat out for a short period of time is part of an illustrator's life. Of course one cannot go on like this indefinitely but then one rarely has to and, as has been said before, working intensely and quickly can produce excellent results.

Another reason for careful consideration is how appropriate the work is for you. All illustrators enjoy working with specialized subject matter. Indeed illustrators often become known for tackling certain themes; rather like actors being typecast, artists are often offered similar commissions and this can be both useful and exasperating. However, it is important to recognize before accepting work that it is within one's capabilities.

Taking on a commission when one knows that one is going to struggle with the subject matter is asking for trouble. For example, many illustrators have difficulty in drawing the human figure. If your commission requires not only this but accuracy in providing a variety of subtle facial expressions (many 'readers' do indeed demand this level of drawing), then the commission is likely to be difficult, unpleasant and extremely stressful. If the commission is done badly then it is unlikely you will be given further work and there will be the misery of knowing that you have not produced very good illustrations. Saying 'no' might have been wiser.

FEES AND PAYMENT

The fee offered for work is often a source for internal debate and often, sadly, a reason for saying 'no'. In an ideal world one

Four-legged monster by Rina Donnersmarck.

would hope for a reasonable fee relating to the amount of work requested but this is often not so. The fees offered to illustrators working in children's publishing are extremely variable. Sometimes one is offered a royalty and this might impact the advance; sometimes illustrators are offered a flat fee and sometimes a fee only payable on publication.

When one is offered a flat fee this means that the payment for the work will be this one fee. However well the book does, or however badly, one can expect no further payment. Usually one is offered a flat fee on books where the print run is large. The books might retail in a supermarket or chain of shops where the sales are reasonably predictable. The flat fee may be offered to the illustrator in instalments. A flat fee payment will usually be greater than an advance on a royalty.

When one is offered an advance on a royalty it means exactly that: no further money from the royalty will be paid until the advance has been earnt and paid off. It is worth saying here that one sometimes (even usually) does not make much more on the book than the advance, but equally, one is almost never asked to pay back an unearned advance.

The advance is often payable to the illustrator in instalments. The first instalment is paid when the contract is signed and the work has started; the second usually when one hands over all of the artwork; and the third on publication of the work. Publi-

cation of the work, especially if it is a picture book, can be years in the future so one needs to bear this in mind when one is reading the contract. Many illustrators, myself among them, try to arrange for the final instalment to be paid on receipt of artwork and I have to say rarely is this not achieved. It seems extremely unfair that an illustrator who has satisfactorily completed the commission should be asked to wait (sometimes) several years for payment. One would find this unbelievable in almost any other profession – it would equate to a gardener saying, 'I will only pay for these bulbs when I have seen them flower!'

If you are offered a royalty then it is probable that the book is unlikely to make a huge amount more than the advance on the royalty. One is sometimes pleasantly surprised here but, more usually, one is not, so keep this in mind. The royalty is usually between two and five per cent unless the artist has written the book as well, in which case it is double this.

Books are nowadays printed in small print runs and often have a short life. A publisher is often very glad to clear the first edition and reluctant to re-print unless the book has been very successful. Of course if you are Roald Dahl then this is a very different scenario. It is as well going into the business of producing a picture book knowing where one stands; one probably does not become a children's book illustrator for the money. All the same if one is going to try and earn a living out of it then

A double-page spread from Sarah Dyer's book, *Monster Day at Work.*

one needs to have some business sense when negotiating a contract.

Try to have an idea how long the work will take you to complete. Experience tells here but even an illustrator fresh from art school will have some idea of how fast or slowly they work. Comparing the time it will take you to do the work with the fee will give some idea of how well (or probably how badly) you are going to be paid. Another approach is to work out how many illustrations are required and then divide the fee accordingly. This will give you a fee for each illustration and this is often a great negotiating tool when agreeing a contract. Usually a larger body of work is less well paid than a single piece but the amount of work in the larger project, partially makes up for this, or so it seems.

Public lending rights

Public lending rights are available to illustrators and authors who have a published book available for borrowing from the library. One needs to register to qualify for this and it is well worth doing.

The money payable is calculated by determining how many times your books have been borrowed from selected, constantly changing, token libraries. The fees are totalled and paid out once a year. This is a welcome and useful service. One can get an idea of how popular one's books are by how well they do in the PLR stakes. This is especially pertinent because, unlike when a book is purchased, the children themselves are usually left to choose the library books they want. I am frequently surprised how well various books do on the PLR scheme and this leads me to question firstly publishing marketing strategies when selling books but secondly to whom one is aiming the book – the child who reads it or the adult who buys it.

Copyright

When offering a book for publication the copyright is automatically yours unless you give it up.

There are occasions when a publisher may wish to own the copyright and this is a matter for the individual. In these cases the illustrator is paid for giving up these rights. This most usu-

ally happens when one is working for a big organization where the book run is guaranteed to be very large. A well known chain of shops or supermarkets often demand copyright. They may publish many thousands of books that sell in their stores and perhaps they wish for the option of producing 'spin-off' items like soft toys, clothing or colouring books without the complication of having to obtain permission and negotiate additional fees. This is something that one should be aware of before signing the contract and as, has been stated, it is up to the individual as to what terms are agreed. One always has the option of declining the work if one is not satisfied that the contract is fair.

THE LONG HAUL

Working and surviving as an illustrator demands ambition, tenacity, a little luck and a great deal of determination. It is an extremely competitive field that is constantly changing and evolving. One needs to be creative and good at having ideas, good at working under pressure, focused and self-disciplined, and one needs to be absolutely sure that one wants to do it. Being a successful illustrator is as much about self-promotion and being pro-active as it is about being able to create good illustration. Of course, if one joins an agency and acquires an agent they will do this for you. If one is on one's own then keeping oneself 'visible' as an exciting and available illustrator is vital. Very often the time when one most needs to do this is when one is busy. Trying to ensure a continual flow of commissioned work rather than waiting until one has no work, and then looking for it, may seem an obvious thing to point out but many illustrators forget in the euphoria of working that this work will come to an end.

Very often projects will take a while to come to fruition. By this I mean that a project first discussed as a possible commission in November may take until the following June to actually get off the ground. In this time there might have been meetings, sample illustrations requested and supplied, it might have been over to the children's book fair in Bologna, to gauge the reaction and 'test' the water, all before a contract was issued. It is worth saying that many books will fail at one of these hurdles and therefore are never realized as a live project at all. That one needs confidence in one's own work and a positive attitude goes without saying. Without them one would soon give up or probably never even start.

PROFILE: RINA DONNERSMARCK

Rina Donnersmarck lives in Bavaria and London and has worked on a huge range and variety of projects, including shop installations, editorial illustration and three-dimensional pieces. Here she talks about how she keeps motivated and creative and the ways in which she gets work.

As a child I used to draw all day long but I always wanted to be a writer or a gardener or a bus driver. There were not too many female bus drivers around at that time so I somehow thought this would make me special. I kept with the drawing and went to art school which, I think, for me was counterproductive. Art school is great for meeting people and learning about new techniques but I think it can totally destroy your creativity. I did not enjoy drawing after I graduated for a long time, but luckily through discipline and some interesting projects, I found my way back into it. It took me many years after leaving art school to return to the way I used to work, my own style before I went there.

The thing I like about working, as an illustrator, is that with every new project comes a new challenge. The constant process of learning and discovering new things, it never becomes boring. I like the fact that I can work from home, locking myself away and getting lost in my own little world.

I think it is essential to have a website. Clients

Rina Donnersmarck.

rarely invite you to come in or want to see your portfolio without seeing your website first. It is convenient and less time consuming for the clients and one needs to keep the website constantly updated. I have an agent who constantly updates my work and my profile and this is what I show to potential clients. The website needs to be clean, interesting and user-friendly, and not overloaded – I would say that this was essential. It is very time consuming to keep it updated and it is not something I enjoy doing much but I know I must.

When I first left art school I got a most of my work by word of mouth. Originally I did not want to have an agent, as I like choosing my own projects and being flexible about when and what I worked on. I did OK without one and of course it is an advantage not having to give away a cut of the money I was earning, but then a good friend of mine started her own agency and asked me to join.

Having an agent enables me to reach parts of the industry that would otherwise be difficult to get into: advertising and publishing for example. Also it enables me to get on with the creative part, the part I like, and not have to worry about the business side, contracts, invoices and promotion. It is useful having an agent in a different country from the one that you are based in because you can reach a much wider audience. Some of my work might not go down so well in the UK market but might be really popular in Japan or somewhere else. A good agent will be aware of this.

Another good way of generating new work is to stage exhibitions. Setting them up can be expensive and hard work but a lot of fun too! Going through all of your old work can spark ideas for new work and projects. It is exciting to let work escape from drawers and see it in the light again. I can see my work afresh like this and can get useful criticism from people who usually don't come across my work unless it is in a public space.

When working I like to try new media but I usually return to pen on paper. I start with quick rough pencil sketches and then begin to think which medium suits this project best. I try to avoid the computer as much as I can and use it only to add final touches or to make small changes of composition, etc.

I am happy and at peace when I am drawing but

it's the ups and downs that keep it interesting. Some days the illustrations come easily and other days it takes many versions to get it right. It can be very frustrating, sometimes not finding the right solution. Usually when I am just about to give up I try to get my senses together and either do some quick research, or experiment with techniques. Sometimes I have a short nap or break or start doodling things that don't have anything to do with the subject and suddenly, out of nowhere, comes the solution. I love these moments and funnily enough, in the end, the simplest and strongest ideas often come from a long struggle, and this is often the work I am most satisfied with.

When working on a longer project it is beneficial to step away from your work every now and then. Getting out of the house, or seeing an exhibition, can recharge your batteries and do wonders for your motivation.

I am interested in illustrators who have found their own language or get lost in their own imaginary world. Ivan Biblin's illustrations of Russian fairy tales, which I remember from childhood, have influenced my interest in more elaborate, detailed and decorative work. Tom Ungerer's children's books stimulate my interest in the darker side of things. Saul Steinberg has the ability to say so much with so few lines and also uses these lines in the most imaginative sense he reminds me again and again that it is best to keep things simple. Baxt's colourful print designs and his dynamic illustrations for the Ballet Russe have beautiful movement and energy to them. His vibrant colours feel surprisingly modern.

Seeing your own work published, after going through such a long process to get to this stage, is very rewarding. It is nice to hold the final product in your hand and it is great to come across your

In this wonderfully decorative and striking illustration of a forest, Rina Donnersmarck uses black and white to brilliant effect, creating an image that is both dramatic and intriguing.

work unexpectedly sitting on a shelf in a shop. I would say never give in a choice to a publisher if you are not one hundred per cent sure about one of them because you can guarantee that this will be the one they choose. I do feel that I am really lucky to have been able to turn what I like doing best into my profession.

PROJECT TWENTY-FIVE: PORTFOLIO PREPARATION

Getting together a portfolio of your work for when and if you visit a publisher is a necessary part of being an illustrator. An A2 portfolio is big enough. Any bigger and it is going to be troublesome to carry around; furthermore it will be awkward to open it in a small office space. However, today, when publishers initially view work online, on websites, if you are taking a portfolio then one wants to include in it 'real' artwork. There is never any substitute for seeing the real thing. Therefore a portfolio filled with copies might be deemed disappointing, in which case you are unlikely to want a portfolio smaller than A2. Fill the portfolio with around ten plastic sleeves. This is enough. More than ten sheets will dilute the quality of your work and could become tedious. The portfolio is a taste of what you do, not the life and times of ... !

Line the sleeves with black or white sheets of thin card or paper. I prefer white as I think it better sets off the work giving it a fresher feel, however I accept that this is probably personal taste. Do not use a coloured card for backing. Try not to choose heavy card for this job. The portfolio will be heavy enough without making it more so.

Now assemble examples of your illustrations into the portfolio. Try not to crowd too many images on each page. One or two, if they are small, illustrations for each page is plenty. Putting together a portfolio is very like putting together a book: one needs to think what goes best with what, how the portfolio reads as a sequence of images, and how the double spreads of the portfolio should be designed.

Capturing your client's interest with the opening pages is essential because it is much harder to decide to like something once you have started thinking it is not quite right for you. On the other hand one does not want the portfolio to start off strongly and then gradually fizzle out. If you do not have enough strong work for ten sleeves then fill only five. This will be much better than putting work in that you are not sure about. Try to finish on a strong image as well as the editor may leave the portfolio open here whilst you discuss possible work.

PROJECT TWENTY-SIX: A BUSINESS CARD

We have discussed at length in this chapter different ways of producing a business card. Obviously the main thing is to have a business card in the first place, and secondly to have one that you feel represents you in the way you want to be represented. Whether you use a professional printer or make your own individual business cards, choose an image to go on it that represents the work that you do and would like to get more of. Do not have too many printed as your work will change and you will probably soon want to have a fresh image to represent you. The contact details need to be clear and legible so if you are hand rendering this information make sure it can be read by those unfamiliar with your writing. Believe it or not I have several times been given business cards where I could not read the email address.

In producing an image for your card do not underestimate the possibilities available by cropping and editing out details from larger illustrations. This is a really excellent way of getting a brilliant and intriguing image for your card and often much more successful than producing an illustration specifically for it.

PROJECT TWENTY-SEVEN: DOING SOMETHING ELSE

If you find yourself stuck for an idea, or devoid of creativity, or maybe just struggling with a commission that you are working on, then rather than sit at your desk trying to force something to happen you may find it more useful just to do something else.

Going for a walk, or seeing an exhibition, or even picking up a book is often a better way of getting rid of illustrator's block. Try not to feel guilty just because you are not sitting at your desk. Being able to continually come up with lively and interesting work is difficult and cannot be done in a vacuum. One needs to continually feed this part of the brain. It is a fact that one can most often find the solution to a problem when one is doing something else and not thinking too hard about it. A long walk might be just the thing – but remember to take your sketchbook.

ACKNOWLEDGEMENTS

Firstly I would like to thank Nicki Potter who initially thought of me as a possible illustrator to write this book. Without Nicki putting me forward there would not have been a book, from me anyway.

I would like to thank all of the illustrators who agreed to be in this book. I would like to thank them for their time and trouble in going through the interviews with me, and then sorting out illustrations to include. For trekking all the way out to my studio (James), and cooking me a special vegetarian lunch (Clare), for managing to conduct an interview across continents (Il Sung), and for putting up with my atrocious computer skills and losing everything you sent (Emma), for enduring the appalling tea at the Royal Festival Hall (Wesley and Corban), and for not asking me to come all the way down to Brighton

The Lion and The Tiger by Martin Ursell.

(Sarah), and for having me email you on your honeymoon (Rina) and for interrupting work on your own children's book (Lynn).

I would like to thank Judith Escreet of Frances Lincoln for agreeing to give this book a professional Art Director's insight. I would also like to thank the illustrators Nancy Slonims and Andrew Baker, my Middlesex University colleagues, for their encouragement and scanning masterclasses in getting this book together. Again, without their initial urging that I accept this commission, I probably would never have embarked on this book. Thank you for that, you two! Many thanks also to William Gillingham-Sutton for shedding light where there was darkness. I reckon you gave me a dodgy camera there Will!

Thank you to Emily Hall and Sean Chilvers who, respectively, took time out from throwing pots in Denmark and a frantic Pentagram schedule to introduce me to the wonders of Photoshop and for rescuing the illustrations from my scanning skills ... or lack of. Sean, I think you might still be tweaking these illustrations now had the book not had to go in.

I am sure the manufacturers of highlighter pens would like to thank my wife Anne who read through this entire manuscript, liberally colouring it in with her yellow highlighter pen as she went. Thank you for that, Anne.

Lastly, but most importantly, thank you to the illustrator Carolyn Dinan who not only agreed to write the foreword to this book but also taught me, as a student at what was Chelsea School of Art. I will for ever be in Carolyn's debt. Carolyn is an extremely inspiring, encouraging and influential teacher who has had a hand in the careers of literally hundreds of illustrators working today. Carolyn was, and is, the most marvellous teacher and it is perfectly true to say that without her invaluable advice and guidance I, and many more illustrators, would not have ever been illustrators at all. Thank you Carolyn.

Illustration acknowledgements

Many thanks to all of the publishing houses for allowing their illustrators' work to be featured in this book. Thank you to Barefoot Books, www.barefootbooks.com, for allowing Clare Beaton's work to be reproduced. Thank you to Meadowside Children's Books for allowing Il Sung Na's work to be reproduced. Thank you to Hardie Grant books and Bright Agency for allowing Emma Block's work to be reproduced and to Frances Lincoln and Bloomsbury for allowing Sarah Dyer's work to be reproduced.

The author at work in Switzerland.

ABOUT THE AUTHOR

Martin Ursell has illustrated many books for children including the award winning *Song of Pentecost* by W.J.Corbett. He has illustrated stories by Roald Dahl, Marina Warner, Ted Hughes, Pippa Goodhart and Dick King-Smith and is the illustrator of the best selling Gruesome series. Martin was a regular illustrator for the children's TV programme *Jackanory* and his own story *Hairy Hairy* was televised by the BBC.

Martin's many picture books include *Fred's Garden* by Linda Jennings and a book with best selling children's author Julia Donaldson called *Follow the Swallow*. His work also features in *Alphabet Gallery*, a compilation of twenty-six of the most successful contemporary children's illustrators working today.

Martin is currently a senior lecturer in illustration on the BA Hons degree at Middlesex University and a visiting lecturer on the illustration and animation degree at Kingston University.

His interests include reading, running, and gardening and he grows most of his own food!

This is the sketchbook drawing I was making in the photograph. When drawing on location, especially in a location like this, one has to decide at the outset how much time to spend on a drawing. It took three hours to walk to this spot and of course I will need to walk back and this would be a lot of trouble for one drawing. I would hope to complete six or seven drawings on a day out on location like this. Therefore, to avoid getting carried away I will try to get as much down in thirty minutes as I can. It is this that dictates how I approach a sketchbook drawing.

GLOSSARY

Advance — Payment made by a publishing house to the illustrator.

Artwork — Illustration prepared for reproduction usually without text.

Bleed — The area of the artwork that extends outside the trimmed page size.

Concertina book — A book made from paper repeatedly folded back on itself to form an extended zig-zag.

Double page spread — The area of two pages when the book is open.

Dummy book — An example of a book in exact but rough replica to the anticipated finished printed book.

Endpapers — The opening and closing spreads of a book.

Gutter — Usually 10mm either side of the middle of each double spread.

Half up — The actual page size enlarged by half again.

Layout paper — A special translucent paper suited to making roughs and thumbnails.

Light box — A box containing a light bulb covered by a perspex or glass sheet on which drawings maybe placed and traced off.

Proof — The preliminary impression of a printed book to be corrected.

Reader — A book created to help children read.

Rough — Preliminary drawings for a picture book that explore variations in ideas and compositions.

S/s — Same size meaning to produce artwork at the exact same size that it will be reproduced in the book.

Thumbnail — A small visual or rough drawing.

INDEX

Collage by Lynn Hatzius from *Magic of a Smile*.